Organizing for Accountability is the best definitive work on the issues of integrity and ethics that is available in the nonprofit community today. . . . I pray that this book will become a standard text for every CEO, COO, and board member to have in their libraries and in their hearts and minds.

—**Elvin L. Ridder,** President, Management Development Associates

The lack of accountability in religious organizations, both on the board level and on the level of management, has resulted in scandals that have shaken and disgraced the religious community. If management of religious organizations do not heed the warnings contained in this book, it will be to their peril.

—**Lisa A. Runquist,** Chair, ABA Non Profit Corporations Subcommittee on Religious Organizations

This book is a tremendous practical guide ad   cal needs of any ministry. It is a wonderful tool fo   nel, dealing with ethical issues, procedural quest   and many other practical solutions. The autho   ging questions that ministries face and give mea   to aid managements in making responsible decis

—**Sylvia Nash,** Chief Executive Officer, Christian Management Association

Accountability has been thrust to the forefront of Christendom at this time due to wide breaches of trust by several members of the body of Christ. The sad fact is that Christian credibility has been seriously doubted in the marketplace. Accountability and credibility go hand-in-hand in today's ministries, so I happily endorse Robert and Gerald Thompson's strong message to today's Church.

—**Bob Slosser**, Author, President Emeritus of Regent University

This book, like Queen Esther of Old Testament times, has come on the scene for such a time as this. The authors address this key theme of accountability from platforms of key experience. It is more than a manual or textbook, but rather a clarion call for ethical behavior for all of us in Christian leadership—with eminently practical counsel and challenge.

—**Ted W. Engstrom,** President Emeritus, World Vision

Organizing for Accountability is a book long overdue. I found it to be outstanding from a general perspective—an excellent handbook for the new start-up ministry and an excellent standard against which the old ministry can recalibrate.

—**Nimrod McNair,** Chairman, Executive Leadership Foundation, Inc.

A very practical book useful as a guide to thousands of organizations large and small. The Thompsons have captured the source of ethical management practices. I also recommend this book for Christian managers in the private sector.

—**Dwight H. Swanson**, Retired Chairman and CEO, Iowa Resources Inc.

This book grows out of an impeccable education in corporate law, years of experience in religious, nonprofit management, and extensive research and personal reflection on managing with integrity and accountability. It is *essential* reading for anyone who wants to lead a religious organization in a God-honoring manner; many of its insights are available nowhere else.

—**James C. McHann, Ph.D.**, President, William Tyndale College

Superb advice for those who believe it is their Christian duty to be accountable to both God and man.

—**Robert L. Toms, Sr., Esq.**, Past President, Christian Legal Society

No one likes to talk about accountability, yet we all have to be accountable. Robert and Gerald Thompson have told us how to do it—the right way. They have successfully addressed the most persistent conflicts faced by Christian organizations from a very practical, yet legally precise, perspective. The result is INTEGRITY based on the confidence that we can hold ourselves accountable better than IRS or the media, which is eager to write about our failures.

—**Walter T. Linn, Ph.D.**, Director of Genesis Counseling Services

ORGANIZING FOR ACCOUNTABILITY
How to Avoid Crisis in Your Nonprofit Ministry

ORGANIZING for

How to Avoid Crisis
in Your
Nonprofit Ministry

ACCOUNTABILITY

An essential resource for
board members, donors,
employees, and leaders of
nonprofit organizations

Robert R. Thompson &
Gerald R. Thompson

Harold Shaw Publishers
Wheaton, Illinois

*To our wives, each of whom is named Patricia,
and to Joshua, Billy, Brett, Danny, and Lauren.*

We gratefully acknowledge the special contributions of our good friend,
Dr. John A. Barbour. John simply would not allow us any peace until we
completed the manuscript for this book, which he so expertly and kindly
edited. Without John, this book would not have been possible.

Unless otherwise noted, Scripture quotations are taken from the *Holy Bible,* New
International Version. Copyright © 1973, 1978, 1984 International Bible Society. Used
by permission of Zondervan Bible Publishers.

ISBN 0-87788-629-6

Library of Congress Cataloging-in-Publication Data

Thompson, Robert R. 1930-
    Organizing for accountability : how to avoid crisis in your nonprofit
ministry / by Robert R. Thompson and Gerald R. Thompson.
    p. cm.
    Includes index.
    ISBN 0-87788-629-6
    1. Church finance. I. Thompson, Gerald R., 1953- .
II. Title.
BV770.T56 1991
254.8—dc20   90-49569
                                                    CIP

---

99 98 97 96 95 94 93 92 91

10 9 8 7 6 5 4 3 2 1

Table of Contents

Introduction

RELIGIOUS ORGANIZATIONS PLAY AN IMPORTANT ROLE IN THE shaping of modern society. In the United States alone, there are about 294,000 congregations of Christian churches and Jewish synagogues.* Additionally, there are about 90,000 parachurch organizations operating outside the framework of a formal church structure. Mission societies, campus ministry groups, religious broadcasters, religious publishers, and religious schools may organize as churches, church auxiliaries, or as parachurch groups.

Some people accuse religious organizations of being unaccountable and financially irresponsible. Highly publicized scandals in the past have exposed the pitfalls of weak accountability in the affected organizations. But the truth is, most religious organizations are as accountable and financially responsible as business corporations and government agencies, if not more so. Yet, rightly or wrongly, people often expect religious organizations

---

*Estimate of Independent Sector, a nonprofit philanthropic and voluntary action organization.

to abide by a higher standard than their business or government counterparts. This expectation has subjected religious organizations to increased scrutiny in the public eye.

This book was written to help religious organizations respond positively to scrutiny by discussing how they can become even more accountable and responsible. To aid in this purpose, we sent questions to 254 religious organizations of all sizes. One third of them responded. We sent a smaller number of questions to attorneys, of whom 20 responded. Each religious organization or attorney obviously devoted considerable time and thought to their answers, and many provided a multiple-page response. We also interviewed in person a number of leaders, employees, management consultants, accountants, and attorneys for religious organizations.

The questions and interviews were designed to find out, from a management perspective, what is really going on behind the scenes in religious organizations. Some survey questions focused on the directors of ministry. Of particular interest were criteria for board member selection, director responsibility, ethical duties, and relationships with management. We focused on donor concerns and how ministries use donations. We probed organizational integrity and careers in religious management. Questions also looked at government regulation of religious organizations and public confidence in ministries.

The substance of each chapter is primarily based on the survey responses as well as personal interviews with more than one hundred religious leaders and consultants. The authors have observed and worked with various religious organizations over the years, but this book is not intended to reflect any personal experiences. Certainly, much more in-depth research and study would be useful. This book only scratches the surface of these fascinating organizations whose inner workings even large donors seldom see. Yet, the door to understanding how religious organizations work is now open. And what emerges from the research is both good and not-so-good news.

The *good* news is that many religious organizations have capable leaders and are moving from early entrepreneurial organizations to mature, well-managed organizations that are receptive to making decisions based on biblical values and sound business practices. They have prepared for the coming regulatory storm. They are sophisticated, successful organizations concerned about the integrity of their operations and the maintenance of biblically based personal and corporate values. They highly esteem their employees, honestly pursue religious purposes, properly use assets, and provide an environment of corporate accountability.

It's refreshing to realize that many religious organizations are aware of the need to practice what they preach about accountability, values, and ethics. Others are less sophisticated in their organization and management, but are positively moving toward improving the effectiveness and accountability of their operations.

The *not-so-good* news is this: there are still some religious organizations that function as immature, unfocused organizations, highly resistant to change. They often operate with weak, uninvolved boards that seem unaware of their responsibilities to establish policies and to oversee the organization. Few of these organizations know how to operate within the safe harbors of applicable tax laws and prepare for the impending regulatory storm we forecast. Even some sophisticated organizations lack comprehension of what it means to operate as a tax-exempt religious entity in today's increasingly intrusive regulatory climate.

This book is for the multitude of people who care about, give to, work for, sell to, manage, or are curious about religious organizations. It presupposes that all religious organizations desire to be accountable and financially responsible.

Robert R. Thompson and Gerald R. Thompson

1
The Accountability Crisis

"Is THERE AN ACCOUNTABILITY CRISIS IN RELIGIOUS ORGANIZA-tions?" When asked this question, a well-known religious leader gave this surprising reply: "No, but there would be if the Christian public only knew more about them!" The public, in his opinion, sees only the tip of the iceberg. The Christian public would be appalled, he says, if it really knew about the inside workings of many religious organizations.

This is not to say that most religious organizations lack integrity or accountability. There is no reason to impute bad motives or a deliberate intent to deceive on the part of religious organizations. It is simply that they may not have had to exert any conscious effort in the past to make themselves more accountable. Some merely lack an awareness of how accountability can be keyed into their organizations; they require someone to show them what to do.

Public Credibility

The accountability crisis, to a large degree, is a problem of perception or public credibility. It is not enough for a religious organization to be structured for accountability and operate with integrity. Religious organizations must take positive steps to make the public aware of their integrity. There are more than 300,000 religious organizations in the United States. If even a small fraction of them lack integrity and accountability, that is enough to cast doubt in the mind of the public about all similar organizations. A few bad apples can make the public suspect that the whole basket is tainted. Religious scandals that were hot news across the United States in the last few years have produced exactly this result. Well-known ministries that were widely respected for their operational integrity were, nonetheless, affected by the scandals, and many reported a decline in contributions.

The one that has consumed the most TV news time and columns of newsprint is PTL—the Heritage Village Church and Missionary Fellowship, Inc.—and its corporate affiliate, the PTL Television Network. Highly successful at raising money for a variety of religious purposes, PTL has left a host of disillusioned donors dismayed by the revocation of PTL's tax-exempt status, revelations of excessive compensation, and allegations of securities and solicitation fraud. The vast bulk of the ministry's assets became subject to bankruptcy proceedings and steadily declined in value.

Financial mismanagement is only one aspect of the accountability crisis. Numerous religious leaders also have fallen prey to accusations of immorality and sexual misconduct. In spite of this, some of these same religious leaders have continued undaunted in their ministries. Jim Bakker, although now serving a 45-year prison sentence in Minnesota, has said that he will return to television ministry as soon as he is released from prison. Meanwhile, Tammy Bakker has tried to make a television comeback in Orlando, Florida.

Jimmy Swaggart, after being disciplined for immorality by the Assemblies of God, continued to pastor his church in Baton Rouge, Louisiana. The denomination, acting responsibly to hold Swaggart accountable, suspended his license to preach for one year. Swaggart, however, gave up his ordination in the denomination and terminated his affiliation with the Assemblies of God, one of the largest Pentecostal organizations. Swaggart continues to preach and appear regularly on television, although program viewers and contributors have sharply declined.

George Gallup reported in 1987 that "Church attendance makes little difference in people's ethical views and behavior; religious people lie, cheat, and pilfer as much as the non-religious." So, it appears, do some religious leaders and some religious organizations. Increasingly people are asking if religious organizations are accountable to anyone.

Parachurch Organizations

Another question being asked is whether churches, the mainstay of religious organizations, are now overshadowed by the more visible and media-dependent parachurch organizations. The concern is whether or not parachurch organizations can be held accountable by anyone, since they often lack the denominational infrastructure that holds pastors accountable for their actions.

Stephen Board (then editor of *Eternity)* said in an editorial in 1979 that as parachurch organizations have grown, "church leaders have wondered if the tail has begun wagging the dog." Parachurch groups seem to wield more influence, money, and power than churches in today's culture. Thus, pastors charge them with imbalance, doctrinal indifference, and exploitation of congregations for money and people. "The major criticism, and one that is easiest to make stick," Board continued, "is that they lack accountability to anyone but themselves. Parachurch groups are religion gone free enterprise."

Written more than a decade ago, Stephen Board's observations are highly relevant today. What then can be done about this accountability problem?

Internal Accountability

Many religious leaders, when surveyed in 1989, acknowledged that religious scandals have had a negative impact on their ministries, even though their ministries were in no way involved with scandals. Many ministries reported a decline in contributions following the revelation of the Bakker and Swaggart scandals. Yet, when asked if they thought government regulations should be imposed in order to assure donors that contributions are used properly, not one person said he or she would welcome any new regulations! All who were surveyed favored self-regulation by religious organizations. Yet, if self-regulation fails, government officials may feel obliged to act.

How are ministries supposed to regulate themselves? One of the principal means of regulation is *public disclosure*. But disclosure means more than just an annual financial statement. Disclosure has to do with total compensation, including salary and perks, paid to leadership. It has to do with familial relationships, conflicts of interest, and how the ministry is pursuing its stated purposes. Disclosure relates to budgets, fund restrictions, director qualifications, statements of policy, and organizational structure. In other words, public disclosure has to do with any material fact that any prudent donor wants to know about the organization.

At the same time, accountability is not limited to public disclosure to donors. It is also an internal function, whereby the management makes full disclosure to the board of directors, to auditors, and to legal counsel. Furthermore, accountability demands that an organization have the administrative capability of gathering needed information, evaluating it, and making proper decisions based on such information.

Internal accountability is every bit as important as external accountability. In fact, what donors are told about a ministry correlates to what management itself is telling the organization's board, auditors, and legal counsel. If management is not doing its job, donors will never be told all the facts. Because of that correlation, much of this book is devoted to the rationale for management's adequate disclosure of organizational information. Also included are practical tips and suggestions on how to help move management in the right direction toward accountability.

There is a strong perception, whether valid or not, that religious groups, especially parachurch organizations, are accountable to no one but themselves. Some religious leaders make a point of saying that they are accountable to God or to the body of Christ, but to no one else. Yet, one need only talk to employees, donors, or professionals who service these organizations to know that within them there is an accountability crisis. As University of Virginia sociologist Jeffrey Hadden puts it, there is a "crisis in confidence and credibility" created by the scandals.

The process of moving management toward assuming an accountable stance is sometimes painful and almost always uncomfortable. Some religious leaders avoid full disclosure because they perceive it to be "negative thinking" or "preaching bad news." But this is not so. Full disclosure is honesty, integrity, and fairness. When making an investment, no one wants to hear only the salesman's puffing without a fair assessment of risk. Yet some religious leaders only present donors with "victory" stories about their ministry. They never present a straightforward statement of risks and benefits. This is not an honest approach, and it can boomerang and precipitate an accountability crisis.

Enhancing Your Reputation for Accountability

The following chapters will help a religious organization take steps to enhance its reputation for accountability. These steps are prac-

tical and workable; they are not unduly burdensome on management, nor will they make administrative costs skyrocket. In most
cases, once full disclosure is made, a religious organization will
see direct results. Management will run more smoothly and donor
confidence will increase. No guarantee can be made that contributions will increase, but accountability makes a ministry more
responsive to God's leading. And, after all, isn't that what doing
the Lord's work is all about?

Although there are many ways in which accountability can be
enhanced, a majority of problems can be handled by focusing on
the accountability of a religious organization to three groups: an
independent board, donors, and government. Let's look at each of
these three areas in some greater detail.

Accountability to an independent board

When it comes to internal accountability, nothing is more important than a properly functioning board of directors or trustees.
Unfortunately, many people are unsure what the role and function
of a board of directors or trustees is. Does the board understand
and accept its responsibilities to establish policies and to provide
corporate oversight? Does the board ask questions and, when
necessary, demand answers? Is the ministry leader accountable to
a no-nonsense board, or is the board a passive group consisting of
family members and friends?

The downfall of PTL and its president Jim Bakker was fully
covered by the media from April, 1987 into 1990. Obviously, PTL
lacked a responsible board of directors. According to the Septem-
ber 8, 1989 edition of *The Charlotte Observer,* Ernie Franzone, a
former PTL board member, astonished onlookers at the Jim Bakker criminal trial by his lack of knowledge about what went on at
PTL. He testified that he did not know anything about PTL's
deteriorating financial condition, about Jim Bakker's six-figure
salary and bonuses, or about the number of lifetime partnerships
PTL issued. Franzone said he had complete trust in Jim Bakker

and Richard Dortch and explained his failure to ask pertinent questions by saying, "It was the first board I was ever on. . . . With all the positive things going on I just didn't feel that I had reason to question, right or wrong."

Don George, another former PTL board member interviewed by *Time* said, "We directed very little, but we approved a considerable amount." The PTL board ignored its responsibilities by going along with whatever Jim Bakker proposed without asking whether it was right. That board failed in its duty to make prudent decisions, refused to inquire diligently into management's activities, and failed to make its president fall in line. PTL was not a religious organization that knew how to hold management accountable.

The board of directors plays a vital role in a religious organization and is responsible to be a check on management. Too many religious organizations are loosely knit structures governed by an all-in-the-family board or an approving rubber-stamp board.

When asked what things are the most important for donors to know about the management and operation of a religious organization, Dr. James C. Dobson, president of Focus on the Family, said donors need to ask three important questions: "First, is accountability built into the structure of the organization? Second, is there an independent and competent board? And third, is the board really in charge, not just a group of approving observers or well-wishers?" Dr. Dobson is right-on. That's exactly what is needed in religious as well as other nonprofit organizations today.

Jerry White, author of *The Church and the Parachurch: An Uneasy Marriage*, addresses this subject. He notes that "accountability varies greatly from organization to organization. Some have active, involved boards, others have passive, permissive boards." Larger religious groups tend to have checks and balances within their own staff. The smaller groups often have greater freedom, but less accountability. The policies of voluntary financial accountability groups have a restraining and standardizing effect on member organizations, especially in financial areas. "But this still does not speak to the need for accountability in effectiveness of ministry. Who determines whether or not a group is effective?" Who indeed?

Q City Church was founded largely by the efforts of Pastor Smith. The church board is made up of members of the church elected by the congregation. However, the practice has been for Pastor Smith to personally approve each board nominee before the congregation is allowed to vote. As a result, the board is composed of friends of Pastor Smith, who act as little more than a rubber stamp to approve or affirm his every action. If the board wants to become more accountable, what choices does it have?

A The board could allow this practice to continue unchanged. Or, the board could act to delegate all nominating control to a board appointed committee. The second option is more likely to hold Pastor Smith accountable for his leadership.

Accountability to donors

Religious organizations are a powerful growing force in society. Charitable organizations of all types, including churches and parachurch groups, annually receive contributions in excess of $100 billion. This represents about 2.1 percent of the gross national product—and the amount grows each year. Of this total charitable giving, about 47 percent is given to religious organizations. Individuals contributing modest sums carry the weight of charitable giving. While corporations and foundations are generous contributors, individuals outshine them overall by contributing about 83 percent of all charitable giving.

Collectively, and in some instances individually, religious organizations are a powerful, influential, and wealthy segment in society, even though there are numerous small ministries that survive on a day-to-day basis. For example, the top television ministries are experts at fund solicitation. Many of them employ polished and costly sales techniques to raise millions of dollars. Once someone donates to any of these religious organizations, that person's name is entered on a mailing list. From then on, the donor is virtually deluged with fund appeals.

It's time to ask whether religious organizations, churches, and parachurch groups, large and small, are accountable organizations. How efficient are they in the use and application of their resources? Do they use their contributions wisely? Are they what they profess to be? What is the guiding vision for their organization and is it attainable? Has their vision been validated? Are their fund solicitations honest, based upon genuine need and opportunity, or do they seek to manipulate people by means of fear, guilt, or greed? Is the organization true to its image and accountable to its donors?

Organizations without responsible boards hardly instill confidence of accountability in donors. After all, donors have a moral right to know how their money is being spent and whether it actually produces the claimed result. The stewardship of giving is directly related to the knowledge donors have of how contributions will be used. An uninformed donor cannot be a stewardly donor before God, because he or she may be throwing money down the drain.

Some religious organizations appear to be operating in an accountability vacuum where there is little financial, fund-raising, management, or mission accountability. In these organizations, everyone seems bent on doing his or her own thing without having to account to anyone else.

Where faith for the impossible is exercised, there is often an absence of purposeful planning. As a result, contributions may be poured into poorly defined projects of uncertain value. The stated objectives of religious organizations may be commendable. However, lack of management accountability wastes assets—including personnel, contributions, property, and information—and encourages ethical shortcuts.

The president of a management consulting firm representing many religious organizations says, "A lot of religious organizations seem to be threatened by the issue of accountability. I hear all the time, 'If the Lord is in it, why should I be concerned if it's really working or not?' " But management is responsible for the prudent use of an organization's assets! Management must be concerned if something is working or not and not excuse the lack of diligence by blaming it on God. This is a responsibility management owes to the organization's members and board of directors.

There is also a noticeable increase in the concerns of donors about how their contributions are solicited and used. This concern may turn out to be the motivating factor moving religious organizations toward accountability who otherwise neither see nor hear any reason to be accountable. Until they become aware of donor concern, they may not be moved to base decisions on biblical values or to begin to operate ethically.

Q Evangelistic Association invites a well-known speaker to address a meeting of students. During the meeting, a free-will offering, which raises $500, is taken to assist the speaker in his ministry. Past free-will offerings for other speakers have averaged around $300. An employee of Evangelistic Association suggests it would be unfair to pay this speaker an excessive amount compared to others. What should Evangelistic Assocation do?

A Evangelistic Association could pay the speaker $300 and keep $200 for its continuing ministry purposes. Or, Evangelistic Association could pay the entire offering to the speaker. Assuming that in any event the donors will not

be informed how much of the offering has been paid to
the speaker, which action shows a greater accountability to the donors? Paying the entire offering to the
speaker—because donors chose to give their money
specifically to that speaker.

Accountability to government

Religious organizations employ thousands of workers and purchase enormous amounts of goods and services for consumption
and distribution. They fill the airwaves with their messages and
appeals, seeking to influence the way people think, spend money,
view their world, relate to God and to each other, and vote.
Although their religious doctrines and biblical perspectives may
differ, most religious organizations attempt to fulfill their religious
purposes with integrity. Part of the problem, however, is that
proper intent or good faith may not be enough.

Yet, do they check to see whether their good intentions are
meeting objective standards of integrity? When discrepancies are
found between what is intended and what actually results, do
ministry leaders correct the problem? How effective are organizations in the accomplishment of their religious purposes? Do they
scrupulously avoid showing financial favoritism to insiders? Are
they dominated by runaway leadership that manages the organization's assets to massage their egos or for private advantage? Is
the organization prepared for the approaching governmental regulatory storm?

There is little question that Congress, the courts, and the Internal
Revenue Service are fed up with religious organizations that engage
in substantial business activities unrelated to their defined purpose.
Improper fund-raising practices, kickback credit card programs,
excessive lobbying, involvement in political campaigns, and the
diversion of funds to insiders in the form of excessive compensation
or perks are coming under governmental scrutiny.

Not many religious organizations engage in such practices, but unfortunately some do, and they are skating on the thin ice of fraud and nonexempt activities. This, in some cases, is as much due to ignorance as deliberateness. Nevertheless, one wonders whether these organizations could continue their ministry apart from their questionable practices.

These practices underscore the fact that the boards of some religious organizations are not doing their job. Such boards consist in many instances of well-intentioned members who sincerely desire to contribute their wealth, influence, and time. But they are ignorant of their responsibilities, of tax traps for the unwary that can sink a religious organization, and the need for biblically based decision making. It is important that boards of religious organizations assert their power to govern and impose standards of accountability.

Americans are witnessing the early stages of an intrusive governmental regulatory storm that threatens to engulf religious organizations and will likely affect the way they pursue their religious purposes. There will be increasing argument regarding constitutionally based claims as the government seeks to impose greater restrictions upon religious activities and religious organizations. While government should not interfere in matters of religion, the insulation afforded by the constitutional guarantees of religious liberty is likely to be stretched thin, exposing religious organizations to further governmental intrusion.

In a recent opinion of the U.S. Supreme Court in *Employment Division, State of Oregon vs. Smith,* April 17, 1990, a six-justice majority declared that "when religious rights clash with the government's need for uniform rules, the court will side with the government." This new perspective of the Court has the potential to replace the former rule, which had limited government from intruding into the religious arena unless it could assert a compelling governmental interest. While the former rule also had its faults, this new liberal approach could permit an even more serious infringement of religious rights.

Q Media Ministry operates a number of radio and television stations that feature its original religious programming. In order to gain extra protection in the event of a tax audit, Media Ministry claimed church status during its first five years. Then, when it wanted to engage in some lobbying activities, it claimed it was not a church. Now, some time later, the solicitation practices of Media Ministry are being investigated. What choices does Media Ministry have?

A Media Ministry has two options: 1. They could claim church status again if it serves an advantage in hampering the investigation, or 2. they could maintain a status consistent with earlier representations. The second option shows more accountability to government and is more likely to create good will toward public officials.

The religious scandals of the past few years have not helped to establish public confidence in the accountability of religious organizations. The reason for this is quite simple: the perception of the public—confirmed by many religious insiders—is that religious organizations are unaccountable. Religious leaders also are often perceived as lacking ethical moorings, determined to do whatever they desire, regardless of the law or common sense.

This public perception must change, but it will only change as religious organizations and their leaders first accept the reality that they must be accountable. Second, they must demonstrate by action and not by words alone that they will be accountable, that they are concerned about value-based decisions, ethical business practices, integrity, and serving the public good. Unaccountable behavior, greed, and self-serving private interests must cease.

Accountability is not served by:

- avoiding a valid contract just because a better deal comes along

- avoiding an obligation because of a technical defect

- buying supposedly donated property through the assumption of the donor's personal debts

- using contributions for nonreligious purposes

- throwing funds down the tube of poor project planning

- puffing ministry results far beyond the truth.

None of these, however, provide any reason to sneer at religious leaders or to hold religious organizations in contempt. Religious organizations, like business and governmental agencies, are not immune to ineptness, fraud, greed, and self-serving interests. Still, they must be preserved. Why? Because, in spite of their imperfections, religious organizations are the best vehicle to collect and apply resources to the task of bringing hope to people. Not only are they the most effective at this task, but they are also the best suited for it. It is not the role of government to carry the message of religion to the people. Therefore, private religious organizations must not only be preserved, but encouraged.

The good news of Jesus Christ must be preached, and disciples must be taught how to win others and send them out to preach and teach others in an ever widening circle. There is plenty of room in this world for religious organizations committed to excellence, but they and their leaders must be accountable. There is no acceptable alternative, and the time to be accountable is now.

2

What Is a Religious Organization Anyway?

- Legalities   - Finances   - Taxes
- Administration   - Record-keeping

P<small>EOPLE WHO WORK IN FULL-TIME RELIGIOUS MINISTRY ARE OFTEN</small> highly focused. They believe in their calling to ministry, they are committed to seeing it accomplished, and they are constantly seeking new ways to minister more effectively. They often leave secular employment and its financial rewards to pursue other values. Most people in full-time ministry view what they do as the most important thing anyone can possibly do. This devotion to ministry is a tremendous asset to accomplishing the goals of any religious organization.

This same devotion can occasionally obscure the legal, financial, tax, administrative, and record-keeping needs of any organization. These areas are the focus of this chapter.

A ministry focus that is too narrow may regard all other vocational goals as lesser in importance or priority. Most ministries acknowledge the need to be mindful of these things, to the extent of hiring professionals to handle their legal, tax, and accounting needs. Yet, many religious organizations get professional help solely from independent contractors rather than full-time professional employees, even when they can afford it.

Some ministry managers have not yet realized that it is their personal responsibility to oversee and manage the administrative tasks of the organization. They prefer to devote their attention exclusively to ministerial tasks. Their personal involvement in administration extends no farther than to delegate responsibility to someone else. Of course the manager retains veto power over everything the professionals recommend. However, managers such as these do not know how to achieve excellence in administration or management. Their expertise and commitment to excellence only reach the ministerial tasks. As a result, the organization and its administration suffer.

A common mistake ministry managers make is to focus on what the ministry organization *does* to the exclusion of what the ministry organization *is*. Not enough attention or commitment to excellence is paid to the organization as a corporation and the kind of maintenance every corporation needs. This frustrates organizational accountability and leads to a kind of corporate identity problem. Everyone knows what the ministry does, but not what it is supposed to be. This identity problem is often most noticeable in the areas of organizational status, nonprofit status, and tax-exempt status.

Organizational Status

There are a variety of legal forms an organization can take, including a *partnership, trust, association,* or *corporation.*

Partnerships
A partnership is, by definition, a form of business association generally unsuited for religious purposes. Its adaptability to

charitable purposes is too low, and the risk of liability to partners is too high. Plus, a partnership does not have a distinct legal existence apart from its partners, while other forms of organization do.

Trusts and associations

Some organizations are merely unincorporated associations, but since this legal form exposes its members to personal liability for association debts, its use is somewhat rare. Some states (such as Virginia) prohibit churches from incorporating, so they are organized as legal trusts or associations. But this is the exception rather than the rule. The legal concepts applicable to these trusts and associations are in many ways very similar to those applicable to a corporation.

Corporations

The most popular form of religious organization by far is a corporation. Therefore, this book will assume corporate status to be the norm for any religious organization. For most purposes, the law treats a corporation as a person, the same as any human being. It has its own name and the equivalent of a social security (taxpayer identification) number. A corporation can enter into contracts, incur debts, and hire and fire its own employees. When a statute refers to a person, it usually includes a corporation.

The corporate form has many advantages. A corporation's debts are not the personal liability of its members. A corporation can have a perpetual existence, sue and defend suits, hold, use and transfer property, and adopt assumed names for conducting business. A corporation can own or control other corporations (usually referred to as subsidiaries or affiliates). A religious corporation can even own one or more business *(for profit)* corporations. In essence, a corporation has its own identity separate from the people connected with it.

All of these benefits make the corporation an effective means by which to carry out religious ministry. A corporation may receive gifts of property, which it can sell for cash without incurring any tax liability for its members or employees. An incorporated ministry can borrow funds to build needed facilities without putting its members or employees at risk. A corporation is simply a legal device or tool by which a ministry can enhance its capabilities and effectiveness.

A corporation also has needs corresponding with these peculiar advantages. These needs arise because a corporation is not an individual, even though it is a legal person. That is, a corporation exists only on paper; it is a legal fiction. A corporation has no tangible existence, as a human being does. The only proof a corporation has of its existence is what exists on paper. Similarly, the health of a corporation is evidenced solely by what is in writing.

For this reason, a corporation must pay attention to its paperwork. Corporate existence, health, status, financial condition, liability, and accountability all depend on written documents. Any incorporated ministry that fails to have a high regard for its paperwork is inviting disaster. Therefore, a low regard for paperwork and its value to a religious organization will lessen the degree of organizational accountability. An organization can prove it made informed decisions and prudent investments, or incurred reasonable risks, only on the basis of its paperwork.

A key component of accountability for any corporation is an effective system of documentation. Without a proper paper trail, it is difficult for anyone to determine who made what decision, based on what information, and who was told about it. As a result, it is difficult to hold anyone accountable for the myriad of decisions every corporation must make.

However, this does not mean the lack of proper paper trails will reduce the potential personal liability of managers. In fact, the opposite is likely. Managers may be responsible not only for their own undocumented decisions, but also for the undocumented decisions of the people they supervise. If no one can tell which managers made which decisions, the trend is to blame everyone for everything. Courts are not likely to let managers off the hook just because no one can tell who gave which orders. It is better to try to leave a good paper trail no matter what the result, than not to try at all.

A board of directors, for example, acts only in the form of a resolution. If formal resolutions are not proposed, debated, and passed, the board has not acted. Moreover, if a resolution exists only in verbal form, every director will have a different recollection of what it was. The virtue of putting resolutions in writing is that it helps end any dispute as to what action the board took. When resolutions are drafted by someone experienced in recording minutes, it also helps end disputes as to what a resolution means. For the person concerned with the potential for director liability, this is all important.

▼

☐ A rule of thumb: Always put it in writing.

▲

Every religious organization should have a clear chain of command and keep permanent copies of letters, memos, and other documents passing up and down the chain. Of course, not everything management does must be written. Some things are not that important.

Occasionally, someone may suggest that sensitive matters should not be written. But be extremely careful about such matters. If this advice comes from the organization's legal counsel, that's one thing. If the advice comes from another manager attempting to cover up his mismanagement, it is entirely different. The same documents that incriminate some people can exonerate others. If you discover mismanagement by someone else, it may be a good idea to document your findings and report them up the chain of command. Otherwise, you personally could be liable for covering up the problem. For the responsible manager, a good paper trail is vital to staying out of trouble for the misdeeds of others.

Q Missions Board has national coordinators who supervise its missionaries in each of the foreign countries where it operates. A national coordinator believes it is advantageous under local law to incorporate separately the operations of Missions Board in his country. However, he fails to receive prior approval for this action and neglects to send a copy of the incorporation papers to Missions Board headquarters. What action should management take?

A Management could decide to ignore this new organization and deal with the national coordinator the same as it had before. Or, management could require full disclosure of the coordinator's actions and enforce policies dealing with the approval, formation, and relationship of affiliated organizations. The latter shows more respect for each corporate identity and a good paper trail.

Nonprofit Status

Though all corporations are created under state statutes, there is more than one way to incorporate in each state. Business, nonprofit, professional, banking, and other specialized corporations commonly are covered by different statutory provisions, although these may overlap to some extent. A few states, such as California, have distinct statutes that apply solely to religious corporations. In virtually all states, the rules for nonprofit corporations are somewhat different than the rules for profit corporations.

Declaring your purpose

Although one can form a profit corporation for any purpose allowed by state law, nonprofit corporations must expressly declare the purposes for which they are formed. All corporations are creatures of limited purposes, but nonprofit corporation purposes are more narrowly construed than business corporation purposes. The purposes of any nonprofit corporation must be carefully spelled out in the *charter* or *articles of incorporation* (a legal statement of purpose or mission) or they will be presumed not to exist. (In this context, corporate purposes do not mean the usual corporate powers, such as the ability to hold property, make investments, and enter into contracts. These are merely the means of accomplishing some end goal. Rather, corporate purposes are the goals themselves, such as advancing religion, providing charity, or operating a school.)

For this reason, a religious organization should closely follow its charter and *bylaws* (a legal statement of procedures). That is, ministry managers should be careful not to conduct operations beyond what the corporate charter and bylaws allow. Unfortunately, a charter and bylaws are the kind of documents people usually think about only when they form an organization. Then they are forgotten. However, should a dispute arise as to corporate purposes, these documents are the first things an IRS examiner or state attorney general would examine.

Defining the term "nonprofit"

What does it mean to be *nonprofit?* The popular idea of a nonprofit organization is one that does not profit from its own operations. Many people do not expect a nonprofit organization to engage primarily in business activities or to derive revenues primarily from business sources. However, this is not a correct view. A profit corporation may show a loss from year to year, yet its status as a profit corporation is unaffected. Similarly, a nonprofit organization may show business profits from year to year without affecting its nonprofit status. Some nonprofit organizations derive revenues solely from profitable business sources.

A better definition for a nonprofit organization is one that does not allow anyone to profit personally from the organization. The people most likely to profit from any organization are its *insiders,* that is, those who control some aspect of the organization. Therefore, the primary concern of state and federal laws is that the organization cannot be used for the personal benefit of its insiders.

All profit corporations have three principal insider groups: the *stockholders, directors,* and *officers.* Key employees and important creditors may also be regarded as insiders for some purposes.

Nonprofit corporations have officers and directors just as profit corporations do. The board of directors of a nonprofit organization may be referred to as a board of trustees, especially among churches. Occasionally organizations use other names, such as a board of regents, to describe the board of directors. But no matter what the name, the task of the board is the same. The similarities between directors and officers of profit corporations and nonprofit organizations far outweigh any differences.

Except for some rare cases, nonprofit organizations (known as *nonstock corporations* in some states) do not have stockholders. They may have members instead of stockholders (although in many cases nonprofit organizations have no members at all). Since stockholders are the legal owners of the corporation whose shares they hold, a nonstock corporation has no owners in the legal sense. A nonprofit (nonstock) corporation simply owns itself.

The stockholders of a corporation may profit from it regardless of whether it has a current profit or loss. Dividends can be paid to stockholders out of either current or past earnings. In some corporations, the stockholders get the benefit of the organization's tax deductions and credits. Additionally, a stockholder may sell his or her stock for a profit, regardless of current earnings (depending only on how much was paid for the stock originally). Or, a stockholder may donate appreciated stock and not only get a tax deduction, but avoid tax on the appreciation as well. Thus, there are many ways in which a profit corporation can benefit its stockholders even when it is losing money.

These benefits of ownership cannot be passed along to anyone in the case of a nonstock corporation. Nonstock corporations cannot pay dividends (credit unions are a limited exception), nor pass along tax deductions or credits to their members. Furthermore, most membership interests cannot be transferred either by sale or by gift. Where membership interests can be transferred no economic benefit is realized by the former member. Thus, a nonprofit corporation usually lacks any means by which members can profit from their membership. This is certainly the rule in the case of religious organizations.

A family operation?

A personal benefit that is sometimes overlooked, however, is the connection between the organization and the family of its founder or chief officer. The danger is particularly high when the wife and children of the founder or chief officer also are employed by the religious organization. Such family members are rarely hired based on qualifications; neither are they on an equal par with other applicants. They are often hired to work at the top of the ministry hierarchy for a good salary without having to start at the bottom for low pay. When an organization allows this to happen, it invites trouble.

The chief danger in hiring the family members of the founder or chief officer is that they will begin to view the organization as a family operation. The family-owned-and-operated business is a cherished way of doing business based on historical examples and the biblical model. But a nonprofit organization is neither capable of being owned nor is it primarily a business enterprise. Family members in key positions of ministry control will unavoidably tend to feel like they *own* the ministry, even though they do not. They will then act consistent with this feeling, even though it is inappropriate.

The family business approach to managing an organization is well suited to a profit corporation, but is totally inconsistent with nonprofit status. The essence of accountability is independence: A board of directors must be independent from management in order to hold managers accountable. Members must be independent to hold directors accountable. Family control, however, usually works against independence; many times it results in significant overlap in the people serving as members, directors, and managers. Thus, the people whose job it is to hold the organization accountable are the ones who benefit most from a lack of accountability.

Q Parachurch, Inc. is a directorship corporation in which the board members elect themselves. The president and founder of Parachurch, Inc. decides to run for political office. He steps down as president, but remains on the board of directors. Because some donors perceive Parachurch, Inc. as lacking effective leadership, contributions decline. What choices does the board have?

A The board could leave the president's position vacant for a year in the hope he will return if he loses the election. On the other hand, the board could begin an immediate search for a permanent replacement. The latter action evidences an understanding that the ministry does not belong to the president, in keeping with its nonprofit status.

Directorship vs. membership
Organizations face additional accountability problems when they are organized as *directorship corporations* rather than *member-*

ship corporations. A membership corporation is one in which the charter or bylaws grant powers to members other than the directors, officers, and employees. Churches are a good example. The primary role of members is to elect the board of directors, who in turn are responsible to establish corporate policy and oversee corporate affairs. This is no small responsibility and members of religious organizations must elect directors capable of doing their job well. To vote for oneself does not lessen the responsibility to be accountable.

The directors of a membership corporation are in turn accountable to the membership. The nature of this accountability is defined by the corporate charter and bylaws and by state law. The remedy for a disgruntled member in most cases is to terminate his or her membership or elect different directors. In unusual cases, a member may call for the removal of directors or exercise other rights granted by the charter or bylaws. Whether directors are accountable to members beyond this will depend on state law concerning director responsibilities.

The members themselves are primarily accountable to each other and the charter and bylaws of the organization. They are accountable to each other in that they must elect directors who will serve the best interests of the organization. They are accountable to the charter and bylaws because that is the source of all membership rights and powers: members can only do what the charter and bylaws allow them to do. They cannot take over the management of corporate affairs. Members do not run an organization themselves, but merely select the people who will.

In contrast, a directorship corporation has no members independent from the board of directors. The board of directors elects its own members, and there are no other members. Many parachurch organizations and charities are good examples. In some cases, an organization's bylaws may recognize the existence of separate membership and director groups, but they consist of the same people. These organizations technically have members, but are functionally the same as directorship organizations: they have no members independent from the directors. In a sense, the directorship corporation is analogous to the closely-held business corporation.

Among parachurch groups, directorship organizations are the rule. Thus, many parachurch organizations are controlled by a small group of people closely associated with the organization's founder or chief officer. This imposes a natural barrier to account-ability in directorship organizations. Since the insiders elect them-selves, to whom are they accountable? To donors?

Although a directorship organization may refer to its donors as members or partners, donors usually are granted no powers by the organization's charter or bylaws. Therefore, unless donors have the right to elect directors or to vote on other matters, they are not members or partners of the organization in any legal sense. This limits the ability of donors to hold directors accountable. The real power of donors is economic, that is, their power to withhold donations rather than to enforce legal claims. However, this has a limited effectiveness unless the board is notified as to why dona-tions have been withheld and the donations at stake are substantial.

Among churches, however, membership organizations are the rule. Churches usually have a membership distinct from the pas-tors, elders, deacons, directors, or trustees who lead the church. Leadership accountability is often maintained by a clerical or denominational infrastructure in addition to membership account-ability. In parachurch organizations both of these are often lacking. Does this make churches more accountable than parachurch groups? Not necessarily.

In hierarchical churches, for example, ministers may feel their accountability runs solely to the national denomination and not to the local membership at all. In other kinds of churches, the accountability of elected elders may be jeopardized if meetings are held only behind closed doors. If no one knows how individual directors vote on any issue, how can they be held accountable for their actions? Thus, churches and parachurch organizations have distinct yet similar accountability concerns. What can be done?

Nearly every kind of religious organization has areas in which it could improve its accountability. This is true whether the organization is a church or parachurch group, or whether it is a directorship or membership organization. Each organization needs to determine its own areas of vulnerability and take steps to improve its accountability.

Tax-Exempt Status

Religious organizations (including churches) need not be tax-exempt organizations. The pursuit of tax exemption is a voluntary choice and religious organizations are free to be taxable if they want to be. Yet most religious organizations not only incorporate as nonprofit corporations, but also apply for recognition by the IRS as tax exempt. Churches need not apply for tax exemption because exempt status is presumed. But we know of no reason why a church could not disclaim exempt status if it wanted to.

Over 61,000 organizations filed for recognition of tax-exempt status in 1987, according to Robert I. Brauer, Assistant Commissioner of the Internal Revenue Service, Employee Plans and Exempt Organizations division. Of course, not all of these applicants are religious organizations. In 1988, the first year in which user fees applied, the number dropped to 53,000 organizations. The user fee is a filing fee required by the IRS when an organization applies for recognition as a tax-exempt organization. The new fee is $375 where the applicant has gross receipts of more than $10,000 annually. For smaller organizations the fee is $150.

Churches, their integrated auxiliaries, and conventions or associations of churches need not file an application seeking recognition as a tax-exempt organization. Organizations that are not private foundations and have annual gross receipts of less than $5,000 are also exempt from this filing. All other religious or-

ganizations seeking recognition of their exempt status must file a
written application. Form 1023, Application for Recognition of
Exemption Under Section 501(c)(3) of the Internal Revenue Code,
is used for this purpose.

The application must be accompanied by a variety of documents including the charter, bylaws, and financial statements. The
financial statements must include a statement of revenue and
expenses for the current year and three preceding years if available, as well as a current balance sheet. New organizations must
file proposed budgets for the next two years. In addition to Form
1023, an organization must also file a detailed statement of its
proposed activities. The burden is on the organization to show that
it qualifies for the exemption claimed.

Reasons for Needing Tax-Exempt Status

From a federal tax perspective there are only two reasons why
religious organizations need exempt status. First, exempt status
allows an organization to issue tax-deductible receipts to its
donors. That is, the donor can deduct his or her contributions for
federal income tax purposes. Second, exempt status allows an
organization to avoid paying taxes on income derived from business activities related to its exempt purposes. Thus, an exempt
organization is not limited to getting revenues from contribution
sources.

An organization does not need exempt status to avoid paying
income taxes on contribution receipts, as some mistakenly believe.
Income taxes are imposed only on *income* and not on other forms
of revenue. For example, income taxes are not imposed on gifts
because gifts are not income. Since a religious organization's
contribution receipts are gifts, they are not income. Therefore,
donations are not subject to the income tax.

There are additional reasons why religious organizations seek
recognition of their exempt status. These include property tax and

sales tax exemptions in some states. Exempt status also helps to qualify an organization for low postal rates, favorable pension plan status, tax-sheltered annuity plans, and exemption from state and federal employment discrimination laws.

In some ways tax-exempt status leads to an increased intrusion of government into religious affairs. Still, Congress left the door of tax-exempt status open to all religious organizations meeting certain tests. The laws of tax exemption do not take into account the religious beliefs advanced by any organization. Tax-exemption statutes are concerned with whether or not an organization exists for an exempt purpose and uses its profits to further its exempt purposes.*

Dealing with the IRS

When a religious organization seeks recognition of its exempt status, it voluntarily submits itself to the qualifying and operational rules of federal tax law. These qualifying and operational rules must be obeyed; they are not mere suggestions. After getting recognition of its exempt status, the organization must tell the IRS if there are any changes in its sources of support, purposes, character, or method of operation. The IRS may revoke an organization's exempt status if any changes occur that no longer support exempt status. The IRS may take this action even if changes are not reported by the organization but are later discovered by the IRS.

Some religious organizations appear not to understand that the IRS has broad authority in the administration of the tax laws. The IRS may revoke a religious organization's tax-exempt status if it fails to follow exemption rules. The recognition of tax exemption is not a basic right that may be demanded by a religious organization. Organizations have a right to avoid paying income taxes on

*For the legal case see Unity School of Christianity v Commissioner (4 B.T.A. 61, 70, 1926).

donations, but this right is not secured by getting tax-exempt status (as discussed earlier). The ability to issue tax-deductible receipts and to shelter related business income from tax is a privilege. And, like any other privilege, what government gives can be made conditional or taken away.

Because the IRS has a duty to enforce compliance with the tax laws, it will aggressively pursue revocation of an organization's exempt status under certain conditions. These conditions require the IRS to believe that an organization is not furthering any exempt purpose or is operating outside of safe harbors. Tax-exempt organizations must be both organized and operated exclusively for exempt purposes. This is a mandatory rule, not a permissive one. This is a basic requirement of tax law and provides the basis for any IRS tax inquiry.

Rules for Remaining Tax Exempt

There are several rules that define what it means to be organized and operated exclusively for exempt purposes. Each of these rules is a standard of accountability to which an exempt organization will be held:

1. The charter must limit the purposes of the organization to religious or other exempt purposes. The charter may simply state that the organization is created exclusively for religious purposes within the meaning of section 501(c)(3).

☐ Alternatively, the charter may contain a more detailed description of purpose such as the following: The primary, exclusive and only purposes for which this corporation is organized are religious ones, to wit: to conduct Christian religious worship and missionary services, to disseminate, teach, and preach the gospel and teachings of Jesus Christ, to encourage and aid the growth, nurture and spread of the Christian religion, and to render Christian service, both material and spiritual to the sick, the aged, the homeless, and the needy.

▲

2. An organization will not satisfy the tests for exemption if the charter empowers it to engage in substantial unrelated business activities. Neither can an exempt organization actually engage in substantial unrelated business activities, regardless of what its charter says. Unrelated activities are permissible, however, if they are insubstantial in comparison with the organization's overall religious activities. However, profits from such activities are taxable at standard corporate tax rates. The rules defining which business activities are substantial and which are unrelated are discussed in a later chapter. Here it is enough to note that substantial unrelated business activities will negate exempt status.

3. An exempt organization is strictly prohibited from having any *private inurement* or personal profits. As discussed above, state incorporation laws impose a burden on religious organizations to limit their purposes and activities, and to prohibit personal benefit. These requirements are mirrored in the federal tax laws applicable to all religious organizations that seek tax-exempt status under the Internal Revenue Code section 501(c)(3). For federal tax law purposes, the personal benefit insiders gain from a tax-exempt organization is referred to as private inurement.

This prohibition of private inurement is strictly construed by public officials and is not dependent upon a finding of *substantiality*. Even an insubstantial amount of private benefit is fatal to exempt status. This rule, however, does not prohibit people from being reasonably compensated by the organization for services rendered or goods supplied. Officers and employees of the organization may be paid a fair wage without violating this rule.

In a religious organization, the people most likely to derive any prohibited personal benefit are its directors and officers, and in some cases key employees. Profits realized by an organization can be paid to these insiders by several means. These include excessive (unreasonable) wages, large bonuses, free or discounted use of corporate assets for personal use (such as cars and condominiums) and lavish business expense accounts.

The PTL case presents a classic example of private inurement paid to insiders. According to the IRS recommendation to revoke PTL's exempt status dated November 13, 1985, $1,469,871.15 was improperly paid to the Bakkers from 1981 through 1983. About one third of this amount was excessive compensation paid to Jim Bakker. Almost half consisted of assets purchased for the personal use of the Bakker family. The rest resulted from expenses incurred for the Bakkers' benefit that served no exempt purpose, the use of PTL funds interest-free, and excessive bonuses paid to Tammy Bakker.

4. The charter of a religious organization must dedicate its net assets to another exempt organization in the event of its dissolution. While it may seem remote that a religious organization will ever cease operations and dissolve, it does occur. The IRS requires such a dissolution provision to make sure the assets are kept devoted exclusively to religious rather than private purposes. The dissolution provision prevents the transfer of exempt assets to anyone other than another exempt organization.

The IRS will accept a provision in the articles of incorporation stating that "upon the dissolution of this corporation its assets remaining after payment, or provision for payment, of all debts and liabilities of this corporation shall be distributed to a nonprofit fund, foundation, or corporation which is organized and operated exclusively for religious purposes and which is qualified as a tax exempt organization under Section 501(c)(3) of the Internal Revenue Code of 1986 as amended."

5. An exempt organization may not allow itself to become an *action organization*. An action organization is one whose purposes and activities are primarily related to the political process. Thus, an exempt organization may not devote more than an insubstantial part of its activities to attempting to influence legislation by propaganda or otherwise. Nor may it directly or indirectly participate or intervene in any political campaign for or against any candidate for public office. Prohibited activities include the publishing or distribution of statements made in connection with a campaign. These activities are further described in a later chapter on IRS land mines.

Q Christian College launches a publishing house to distribute materials written by its faculty members to enhance its academic reputation. However, to get the program started, it publishes books written by outside authors. Five years later, the publishing house is well-known and publishes many famous authors. It is also so profitable that it provides 20 percent of Christian College's annual operating revenues. Is the College still tax exempt?

A The board of regents could accept the recommendation of a professor that its publishing activities serve an exempt purpose. Alternatively, the board might hire a tax expert to advise them of the risks and options available. The second course of action is better calculated to protect the college's exempt status.

▼

Tax Exemption Checklist

☐ Religious organizations exempt from tax under IRC 501(c)(3) must be organized and operated primarily for religious purposes.

☐ An organization claiming church status need not apply for exempt status on Form 1023 and is exempt from filing an annual Form 990 information return. The IRS cannot audit a church except through cumbersome audit procedures. Churches can also provide a rental allowance to their ministers free from any income tax.

☐ Religious organizations claiming *religious order* status need not file an annual Form 990 information return.

☐ Any religious organization may claim church status or religious order status without IRS approval. In doubtful cases, however, getting a private ruling may be advisable.

☐ A church may nonetheless want to get IRS recognition of its exempt status to help it in securing property and sales tax exemptions in some states. IRS recognition also helps in getting low postal rates, favorable pension plan status, the right to adopt a tax-sheltered annuity plan, and exemption from state and federal employment discrimination laws.

▲

3

Avoiding a Corporate Identity Problem

How can you tell when an organization suffers from a corporate identity problem? The problem in many cases is that employees are so wrapped up in what the organization does that not enough attention is paid to what the organization is.

Helpful Hints

Here are some suggestions on how an organization can keep its true character in view.

▌ **Don't disdain the organization's charter and bylaws.**
Remember that old saying, "this is a government of laws, not of men"? The same principle applies to religious and nonprofit organizations. Everyone, including the founder and chief officer, has limits to what he or she can do on behalf of the organization. These limits are found in the organization's governing instruments, the charter (or articles of incorporation), and bylaws. As no

one in government is above the law, no one in a religious organization is above its charter and bylaws. As far as management is concerned, the charter and bylaws are the same as law.

Management may sometimes view the charter and bylaws as a mere legal necessity or technicality. The limits they impose may be regarded as inconvenient to performing effective religious ministry. If this attitude reflects itself in conversation or actions, however, it has a noticeable trickle-down effect. That is, the rest of the employees will mirror whatever attitude management adopts. It is important to cultivate a respect for the charter and bylaws by everyone in the organization. The foundation of accountability is a uniform standard to which everyone must conform. In a religious or nonprofit organization that standard is the charter and bylaws.

■ **Don't expand ministry activities beyond what the charter permits.**

One of the primary purposes of the charter is to state clearly what the organization can and cannot do. The charter usually contains the official mission statement of the organization. Yet, it is not often that a copy of the purpose statement in the charter is given out to all employees. People rarely set out to expand activities beyond what the charter permits, but nonprofit organizations are entrepreneurial in their own way. When a ministry opportunity comes along, people may quickly seize it without checking the charter first. For example, a church charter may devote all of the church assets "exclusively for religious purposes." However, using church funds to build and operate a retirement village may not serve a religious purpose under state law.

It is also helpful to remember that the charter is independent of federal tax-exempt status. Of course, organizations put things in their charters to satisfy certain tax requirements, but federal law does not govern the charter itself. Even though tax laws allow an organization to engage in religious, educational, or charitable activities, it does not mean the charter allows all of these. If the charter is more restrictive than tax laws require, the restrictions must still be followed. Amending a charter is so simple that there is no excuse for failing to adhere to it.

▌ **Don't fail to abide by the procedural requirements of the bylaws.**

Bylaws are notorious for being hidden in some drawer nobody ever opens. The purpose of bylaws is to set up the procedure by which the organization operates. This procedure is not an obstacle to effective ministry, but is an aid to getting things done right. A fixed procedure everyone knows about also helps create realistic expectations of how things will get done. This is essential for good morale among ministry employees.

Another function of the bylaws is specifying which people have certain powers and responsibilities. The actual chain of command and job descriptions of management often bear no resemblance to what the bylaws of a religious organization say. Instead of using something from a form book, management should tailor the bylaws to meet the organization's needs. Then once the bylaws are adopted, follow them. If management changes the chain of command and individual job descriptions every six months, it is likely management accountability is very low.

▌ **Don't lose track of prior decisions of the board of directors.**

Keeping written minutes of board meetings is the best way to remember what specific action was taken. Yet the way some organizations keep minutes, it is difficult to learn anything from reading them. One common mistake is to try to condense a two-hour meeting that covers several subjects into a single page. Everyone knows the board took action on each item, but the specifics are lost. Thus, it is hard to hold anyone accountable for carrying out the board's decisions. Management is accountable in proportion to the specificity of the instructions given.

Another common mistake is to ignore past board resolutions. A properly adopted board resolution is as binding on the organization as the bylaws. It remains effective until revoked or until it expires by its own terms. If no one remembers what actions the board has taken, though, it could produce some surprises. For example, assume the directors authorized a salary for the treasurer last year and a salary for the secretary this year. There could be an unintended result if the secretary and treasurer are the same person. It pays for the board to remember its past resolutions.

▌ Don't adopt Robert's Rules of Order unless they will be followed.

Many organizations adopt the well-known procedure regarding meetings called Robert's Rules of Order as the standard for parliamentary procedure. Yet, people in the organization rarely bother to find out what Robert's Rules requires. This could be a big mistake. Consider the recent case of *Frankel v. Kissena Jewish Center*, for example. A Jewish congregation was taking a vote on whether to retain or retire its rabbi. A dispute arose about whether proxy votes (the votes of members who were not at the meeting) should be counted. Whether the proxies counted or not would determine the outcome of the vote.

Some of the congregants sued the organization to reverse the decision not to count the proxies. Since the organization's bylaws adopted Robert's Rules of Order to resolve parliamentary questions, the court said Robert's was binding on the congregation. As it turns out, Robert's disallowed proxy voting. The congregants who sided with the proxy votes were not pleased, and they lost the case. If someone had bothered to check Robert's Rules before the meeting, the vote may have come out differently.

■ **Don't overlook the need for full-time administrative personnel.**

Most religious organizations employing more than just a handful of people have management needs best served by full-time professional administrative employees. There are endless regulations pertaining to corporate filings, tax return preparation, and accounting procedures alone. No one but a professional can keep track of them and hope to stay in compliance. And, as any organization with a sizeable mailing list knows, in-house computer programming and expertise is a necessity, not a luxury.

It simply is not realistic to expect people lacking professional business training to handle complex administrative tasks. Yet some organizations expect employees with little or no administrative training or experience to handle every aspect of administration competently. One way to supplement the administrative competence of an organization is to hire outside consultants. This avoids the need to hire full-time professional administrators to some extent. It creates other problems, however, as discussed below.

■ **Don't rely solely on outside consultants for professional advice.**

The administrative staffing problem is not solved by relying exclusively on outside professionals for advice. Outside professionals have other demands on their time that prevent them from knowing the inner workings of the organization in detail. Therefore, they have a limited ability to discover the problems that exist and bring them to management's attention. It is not a question of whether they will give better or worse advice than in-house professionals. It is simply a recognition that outside professionals cannot advise about things they do not know exist. Outside consultants are best used as an adjunct to in-house administrators, not as a substitute.

Among administrative staff, accountants and lawyers are some of the most important. Having in-house legal and accounting counsel is the best way to introduce some significant account-ability structure in any organization. Not all tactics are equally suited to carrying out ministry goals. Accountants and lawyers have the ability to view ministry operations from a business perspective. They can then suggest alternatives that accomplish the ministry goals but avoid the problems. This perspective is also invaluable in spotting potential financial disclosure problems.

▌ Don't overlook the spiritual aspect of administrative work.
Administrators do more than just enable ministerial staff to carry out their ministry. Administration and management are actually forms of spiritual service in their own right. The Bible recognizes the gift of administration in 1 Corinthians 12 and the gift of leadership in Romans 12. In 2 Corinthians 8, Paul refers to the administration of ministry as being "to honor the Lord himself" (verse 19). He goes on to say, "We want to avoid any criticism of the way we administer this liberal gift" (verse 20). Administration and management are as valuable to an organiza-tion as its ministry.

Administration and management, then, are not spiritually neutral. There are right and wrong ways to administer. It should be as important for an organization to carry out a correct view of administration as it is to carry out a correct view of ministry. Proper administration is the key to improving organizational account-ability. It also recognizes the division of labor that is divinely distributed among believers. Until an organization realizes that some ways of doing things are better than others, and then commits itself to doing what is best, accountability will never improve.

▌ Don't overlook the need for a well-defined chain of command.
Another key to organizational accountability is a well-defined chain of command. Accountability is not just a concern for upper

management, but for everyone who works in a religious organization. Every employee and staff member should report to someone else in the organization for accountability purposes. Without this essential management structure, it is impossible to maintain good employee job performance and ministry integrity. And unless this chain of command is plainly communicated to everyone, it will not work.

Religious organizations must be careful to hold their own employees accountable to avoid undesirable government intervention in this area. Ministry self-government is not only a virtue, but a practical necessity. Matthew 18 shows how churches are to hold their own members accountable in the case of misconduct. In effect, grievances and discipline are effected through the chain of command, with appeals working up the chain. This same principle applies to all religious organizations, regardless of their form. A well-defined internal management structure is as important to any ministry as the external structures of nonprofit corporation law and the tax laws.

■ **Don't place convenience above obedience to various laws.**
Organizational formalities are especially important when a recognized nonprofit tax-exempt ministry forms an offshoot group. When a church forms a "sister church" intended to be separate, it should be separately organized from the beginning. The new church should not deposit donations into a bank account in its own name until after it has been separately organized. Nor should it borrow the other church's tax-exemption numbers after it has been separately incorporated. Also, Sunday school classes of recognized churches should not open their own bank accounts except in the church's name. Otherwise, the class may be viewed as a separate organization that is for profit and taxable.

A ministry is not a nonprofit organization merely because its organizers intend for it to be so. Nor is a ministry tax exempt merely because it is nonprofit. Unless a ministry is organized under a state nonprofit corporation law or its equivalent, and the proper filings are made, it is not nonprofit. Unless a ministry files an application for tax exemption with federal and state agencies, it is not tax exempt. An organization must go through these inconvenient formalities, or it is presumed to be for profit and taxable. Reports and applications take time and money to prepare and file, but they are important.

4

The Key to Organizational Accountability

As EVIDENCE OF INSTITUTIONAL FAILURES KEEPS POURING IN, IT IS clear many business and nonprofit organizations are in trouble. The principal reason: management lacks accountability to an independent, informed, and involved board of directors.

The *Business Week* article quoted above adds, "The list of board failures could go on. It would include much of the savings and loan industry, which has been riddled with unscrupulous practices and unwise lending policies. Then there are defense contractors, also rife with scandals that boards might have prevented or squelched." Add to these the religious ministry scandals that exposed prominent ministers as men who treated donor-financed assets as their own. Meanwhile, the boards of these organizations approved just about everything their leaders proposed.

Why have boards of directors not fulfilled their duty to govern organizational affairs? Why do boards seem unconcerned about the best interests of the organizations they serve? Why are many boards passive and uninvolved? These questions are the same for both business corporations and nonprofit organizations. Boards are ultimately responsible for exercising all organizational powers and managing all organizational affairs. Boards are to govern, make prudent policy decisions, oversee operations, and hold management accountable for its actions. Yet, boards of business and nonprofit organizations have not been diligent to do these things. Why?

Is it because these boards lack independence and are mere tools of management? Do the directors believe management is somehow naturally accountable? Is it because they are uninformed about what's going on in the organization and can't see through management's smoke screens? Are the directors unqualified and untrained to exercise their powers? Or are they simply unaware of their duties as directors? In reality, all of these are contributing factors.

Some other factors contributing to board failure are unique to religious and nonprofit organizations. For instance, many nonprofit boards consist of volunteer directors who serve without pay. Such volunteer directors often believe they serve in an honorary and passive capacity. They believe they lack authority to do anything but advise, counsel, and approve. Rarely do they question, challenge, or oppose management when necessary. Yet who do they serve when they give advice or counsel? Sadly, many directors mistakenly think they serve a ministry's chief officer rather than the organization itself. They do not seem to realize they are organizational governors who have certain predefined responsibilities.

The Role of Directors

State laws give every corporate board of directors the duty and power to direct all the affairs of the organization. These laws typically say that all corporate powers shall be exercised by, or under the authority of, the board of directors. Furthermore, the business and affairs of a corporation must be managed under the direction of the directors. The scope of powers and duties granted to boards of religious organizations is fairly uniform throughout the United States. Their powers and duties are not much different from those applicable to the boards of business corporations.

Although the powers granted to a board of directors are broad, they are not unlimited. Boards work best when they address only policy issues and allow management to carry out the policy decisions. Nothing is more frustrating to management than for a board to intrude into management's sphere of operations. On a practical level, though, it is sometimes difficult to know which matters are for the board and which matters management should handle. Even so, the general rule is easily stated.

In essence, directors are organizational governors or overseers, not managers. That is to say, the board makes policy decisions and management does what is necessary to carry out board policies.

What does it mean for a board to *make policy?* The *New Lexicon Webster's Dictionary* defines policy as "a selected, planned line of conduct in the light of which individual decisions are made and coordination achieved." To make policy means that the board adopts a planned line of conduct, or strategy. Management's job is to decide how best to carry out the board-defined line.

Q Some of the staff of Christian School want to raise money to fund a campus expansion project. How should they go about this?

A Management should recommend that the board authorize a capital funds campaign. If the board has enough information to act, it should spell out the important points of the campaign in a formal resolution and then direct management to carry it out. If the board needs more information, it should direct management

to study the issue and report back to the board with its
findings. At that time, the board can spell out the terms
of the campaign in a resolution and direct management
to carry it out. Management may retain advisers and
consultants in carrying out the campaign so long as they
follow board guidelines.

Thus, the board handles all nonroutine matters affecting the
organization while management handles all routine matters. Nonroutine matters best handled by the board include any change in
legal status or tax status. Examples: corporate qualification, state
licensing, government funding, exempt organization classification, dissolution, merger, bankruptcy, lawsuits, and similar matters
are usually nonroutine. Nonroutine matters also include important
business decisions affecting the entire organization. These would
include moving the principal business office, fund-raising campaigns for capital improvements, launching new ministry activities, selling major assets, or forming related organizations.

Once the board has made a policy concerning any issue, it is
the job of management to make sure things get done. Any decision
on how to carry out the board policy is for management to make,
so long as the board policy is not frustrated.

Q An employee of Media Ministry proposes that the organization sponsor a credit card in cooperation with a
major commercial bank. Under the proposal, Media
Ministry would promote the use of its credit card by
employees and donors. In return, it would receive a one
percent commission on all purchases made by credit-
card users. After looking into this proposal, management
has been advised that this commission is unrelated business income taxable to Media Ministry. May management decide to proceed with the credit card?

A If the board has already adopted a policy against taxable unrelated business activities, management must prohibit the issuance of a ministry-sponsored credit card. If the board has not prohibited such activities, management should seek board approval before launching a credit-card rebate program. Because the decision to engage in unrelated activities is not routine, it is a matter that only the board can decide.

Because boards are organizational overseers and not managers, they should delegate management responsibility to others. In practice, such board delegation is the way most organizations are managed. The Revised Model Nonprofit Corporation Act (see Appendix A) is a model statute proposed for adoption by the states by the American Bar Association. It implicitly recognizes the authority of the board to delegate management responsibilities to others. "All corporate powers shall be exercised by or *under the authority of*, and the affairs of the corporation managed under the direction of, the board." (Emphasis added.)

In fact, the laws of various states do recognize that the board may delegate management responsibilities to others. The California law governing religious corporations states, "The board may delegate the management of the activities of the corporation to any person or persons provided that the activities and affairs of the corporation shall be managed and all corporate powers shall be exercised under the ultimate direction of the board."

The usual recipients of these delegated responsibilities are officers of the organization. The following bylaw provision is an example of how such delegation is often handled: "Directors shall have the power to appoint and remove all officers of the Corporation subject to such limitations as may appear in these bylaws, and to prescribe such powers and duties for officers as may not be inconsistent with law, with the Articles of Incorporation, or these bylaws." Officers are not directors simply because they are also officers, though it is common in religious organizations for officers also to be directors.

Officers are responsible to obey state laws that set forth certain standards of conduct. When officers faithfully fulfill their responsibilities, they are not personally liable for the results of their actions. In addition, officers are accountable to the board. The organization's bylaws recognize this accountability on a practical basis. Bylaws define officer duties and powers in addition to procedural matters. Like directors, officers also are duty-bound to act in the best interests of the corporation.

Nonetheless, the board is legally responsible to govern organizational affairs. Directors, therefore, hold the key to organizational accountability and are its guardians. The board must direct the management of organizational affairs and use its powers to require management accountability when necessary. Nothing is more important to organizational accountability than for the board to assert its power to oversee business and ministry affairs. Even volunteer directors of religious organizations hold the key to organizational accountability.

Is this too much to expect of a volunteer board of directors? Perhaps. But there is no good alternative. Boards of religious organizations should not be done away with merely because it takes time and commitment to be an effective director. Religious organizations would not be more accountable if operated by a highly paid chief officer without a board of directors.

An involved, committed board is the better way to ensure corporate accountability, even though some religious leaders pretend their boards do not exist. A knowledgeable, committed volunteer director can act responsibly and fulfill his or her duties once those duties are known. A key problem with many boards is that directors and management are fuzzy in their understanding of how a responsible board can be the catalyst for an accountable and vibrant organization.

According to the October 9, 1989 issue of *National & International Religious Report*, during the criminal trial of Jim Bakker, former president of PTL,

> directors testified that they had been kept in the dark about finances. They met infrequently, they never discussed questions of importance, they spent little time reviewing brief financial reports . . . They were not told the IRS had warned PTL about the high amount of remuneration Bakker was getting nor were they told the IRS was investigating PTL . . . They were not allowed to take home copies of board minutes or any other PTL documents. Several members were obviously compromised by a conflict of interest: they worked for a PTL contractor or they had received funds from PTL. Experts on non-profit organizations say one of the chief revelations of the trial was the failure of directors to carry out their fiduciary responsibilities.

If the directors of PTL had been properly informed, they could have used their oversight powers and held management accountable for its actions. If PTL's board had all the information it needed, the scandal involving the overselling of lifetime lodging partnerships (similar to time-sharing vacation plans) might have been avoided. In defense of the PTL board, however, the evidence shows that management kept the board ignorant of corporate developments. The management may even have obstructed responsible inquiry and deliberations necessary for the board to fulfill its duties.

Because a board is at the top of any organization's hierarchy, it is best positioned to bring about organizational accountability by persuasion and influence.

A board has both *authority* (the legal right to act) and *power* (the physical capacity to act) to make policies and to oversee ministry affairs. The board has this authority and power to protect, preserve, and promote the interests of the organization. The interests of a religious organization include its relationships with donors, employees, members, and suppliers. An independent and informed board free of conflicts of interest or undue management pressure is vital to encouraging innovation and maintaining accountability.

Dr. Stephen E. Slocum, Jr., President of the American Tract Society, notes the important connection between director independence and accountability. "We look for [board] members who are responsible men or women, with a commitment both to the Lord's work and the Society's role in carrying it out. We do not, however, choose directors according to their ability to be financially supportive. No family members are allowed." In 1987 Billy Graham said in a letter to contributors, "I am thankful that many years ago we formed a strong board of directors to handle our finances."

How a Board of Directors Operates

It only takes one scandal, such as the PTL one discussed in Chapter 1, to show how dangerous it is for a board of directors to assume that management will provide them with all the information needed to make decisions without having to ask for it.

A board cannot oversee organizational affairs and maintain a productive relationship with management unless it makes informed decisions. Directors must get and understand all the necessary information before deciding. This is the only way to make decisions in the best interests of the organization. While directors should not assume management is trying to hide something, neither should they assume they have all the information they need. In many instances, management's failure to provide needed information merely means it does not realize the board requires it. Yet, just to be sure, directors should ask.

While religious organizations differ in their missions, their boards often have one thing in common: They are unaware of their duties and the reasons for their existence. Directors sometimes act as if they do not know they are part of a decision-making body. They may not realize that their unique position in the organization enables them to make policy, oversee affairs, and set accountability standards. To fulfill their duties, the board must ask questions. Directors must ask questions even if the environment is positive and they have a complete trust in management.

The board must have the freedom to discuss and debate issues, deliberate, and then make its decision. The board can make responsible decisions only if it has its eyes open and has access to all relevant information. If management discourages the asking of questions or characterizes reasonable inquiry as negative, directors should resign. There is little other choice. If management refuses to provide answers to reasonable questions, directors cannot fulfill their duties. Then there is no purpose in serving as a director.

Decision making at the board level is hard work. It is a process that requires the asking of questions and an insistence upon answers if necessary. It requires an evaluation of facts and information, a weighing of risk and reward, and a review of alternatives. It may also require consultation with experts such as accountants, attorneys, fundraisers, engineers, and financial planners.

A board needs to take eight steps to make effective decisions:

- ask relevant questions

- evaluate information but do not assume all necessary information has been provided

- examine the known alternatives

- weigh risks and rewards

- seek the opinion of experts

- consider everything in the light of biblical values

- fulfill the organization's purposes

- decide.

Although directors are responsible for making policy decisions, the practice in some religious organizations is quite different. The directors in these organizations are uninvolved, uninformed, and uncaring. The chief officer makes *all* decisions. Yet this is not the way to make decisions. The Bible speaks of wise leaders seeking the counsel of others and the wisdom of diligent planning. The board level is where policy decisions should be made.

Meanwhile, management has a duty to submit all policy issues to the board. Management should provide the board with all facts and information that are relevant to policy issues. They also should disclose all reasonable alternatives and opportunities. Management's duty is to make a full and complete disclosure to the board of everything necessary for the board to make an informed decision.

Dr. David Hubbard, president of Fuller Theological Seminary, has an interesting way of providing the board with all the information necessary to making an informed decision. Dr. Hubbard says,

We share bad news with the board first; we tell 110% bad news and 90% good news in order to compensate for our almost unconscious tendency to cheat. We want to tell the board all the good news, and we want to minimize the bad news—and that is exactly wrong. Ducking controversy or minimizing difficulty, snowing people with reports that are not realistic about the quality of the programs or financial stability or whatever—all of that is terrible leadership.

When directors actively discuss issues, they will occasionally disagree. There is nothing wrong with directors debating the merits of a proposal in this way. This is especially true when the proposed policy involves ethical questions. Directors must have the liberty to debate issues, exchange ideas, gather information, and become informed before they decide. An expression of disagreement is a healthy sign in the board room. It shows that the board is concerned about its duties and cares about the impact of its decisions. A routinely unanimous board may mean that directors are not taking their roles seriously, rather than that they are of one spirit.

The board room must be a forum of free and open discussion. In some organizations, though, a dissenting director is threatening to fragile egos and is characterized as a negative thinker. The rule in these organizations is that God's will can only be discerned when there is a unanimous decision. Such a rule means that healthy, probing questions never get asked. In the end, the expression of different views and resulting creative solutions are discouraged, suppressed, and lost.

The suppression of different views is wrong and works against setting a high standard of organizational accountability. Where only views supporting or approving management are permitted, truth and reality are suppressed. Where differing views are discouraged or characterized as negative thinking, accountability is also suppressed. The result is poor, ineffective, and unaccountable board decision making. The better rule is to encourage an open and free discussion where all views are heard and respected. There is no reason why a split board decision is unacceptable. Where there is freedom to vote against proposals, accountability abounds, and effective, positive board decisions are possible.

The book of Acts relates how the apostle Paul and Barnabas once had a sharp difference of opinion. They disagreed on whether John Mark should accompany them on a return trip to see how the new converts were getting along. Paul rejected the idea and a split decision occurred. Paul chose Silas and went to Syria and Cilicia. Barnabas, however, took John Mark with him and sailed for Cyprus. Although Paul and Barnabas disagreed, it worked out well for both of them. Unanimity was not necessary for the ministry to continue. In fact, unanimity, had it been the rule, would have frustrated any meaningful missionary activity by either Paul or Barnabas.

A caution is in order, however. When the board encourages free and open discussion, deliberation, debate, and even dissent, directors should be on guard. They should avoid approaching every decision from a negative or "thumbs down" perspective. This unduly strains the relationship with management. It also stifles the very thing boards of religious corporations need most—a mutual and open exchange of ideas, opinions, and creative solutions. Directors need to temper the pursuit of honest inquiry with a spirit of cooperation toward management to avoid an antagonistic relationship. When the spirit of cooperation is lost, the organization's management, ministry, and accountability will all suffer.

The Duties Of Directors

It is not easy to govern a nonprofit religious organization because there are few standards by which to measure achievement. There is no bottom line of profit or return on investment as in business corporations. The results are intangible and difficult to quantify. The board, then, has a difficult responsibility to fulfill. Directors are nevertheless accountable to act in the best interests of the organization and they cannot afford to be ignorant of their duties.

Every director occupies a position of trust in a religious organization. This means a director should act in the best interests of the organization, not in his or her own interests. Directors are accountable to fulfill their duties on behalf of the organization under applicable standards of conduct. Every state has specified duties that the directors and officers of business corporations must fulfill. Twenty states have expressly adopted standards of conduct for nonprofit directors and officers. The remaining states would probably apply standards of conduct for business corporations to the directors or officers of religious organizations.

The PTL bankruptcy hearings illustrate this last point. The bankruptcy court said that Jim Bakker (an officer and director) and David Taggart (an officer) had breached their duties to PTL (a religious corporation). The court reached this conclusion by relying upon a South Carolina business corporation statute. (South Carolina does not have statutory standards of conduct for nonprofit directors and officers.) The court then applied this statutory standard of conduct to Bakker and Taggart. The court said that,

Good faith requires the undivided loyalty of a corporate director or officer—and such a duty of loyalty prohibits the director or an officer . . . from using this position of trust for his own personal gain to the detriment of the corporation. In this instance, there are no shareholders of the corporation; however, even though there are no shareholders, the officers and directors still hold a fiduciary obligation to manage the [religious] corporation in its best interest and not to the detriment of the corporation itself.

. . .[T]he duty of care and loyalty required by Bakker and Taggart was breached inasmuch as they: 1) failed to inform the members of the board of the true financial position of the corporation and to act accordingly; 2) failed to supervise other officers and directors; 3) failed to prevent the depletion of corporate assets; and 4) violated the prohibition against self-dealing.

The PTL bankruptcy decision, though not binding on other courts, still serves as a warning to directors and officers of religious organizations. Directors and officers are responsible to act for the corporation's best interests. Courts will hold them accountable to statutory standards of conduct. Without express standards for nonprofit corporations, courts will apply the standards applicable to business corporations. Directors and officers of religious organizations should act in the organization's best interests. They should act in good faith, free of any conflicts of interest and according to recognized standards of conduct. And these standards of conduct will be applied whether directors and officers are aware of them or not.

A business consultant to religious ministries was asked whether the directors of his client organizations understood their responsibilities. He replied, "About 70% of the boards we've seen and worked with see themselves as passive bodies serving for name recognition. They do not realize their responsibilities, and when I've pointed them out some of the directors resigned on the spot."

Directors and officers of religious organizations should fulfill their duties in a responsible manner. California is one of the states that has adopted specific standards of conduct for directors and officers of religious organizations. These duties apply without regard to whether a corporation pays its directors. Section 9241(a) of the California Corporations Code states,

> A director shall perform the duties of a director, including duties as a member of any committee of the board upon which the director may serve, in good faith, in a manner such director believes to be in the best interests of the corporation and with such care, including reasonable inquiry, as is appropriate under the circumstances.

The Revised Model Nonprofit Corporation Act expressly recommends that states adopt general standards of conduct for directors and officers of nonprofit corporations. These recommendations, as shown in Appendix A and Appendix B, are very similar in content to the California law.

The best way to consider these standards of conduct is to look at each of their components. These include the *duty of care*, the *duty of loyalty*, and the *duty of obedience*.

The duty of care

If directors act without adequate information, they expose themselves to possible liability for breaching their duty of care.

Q A donor wants to give some vacant land, which she claims is worth $2.5 million, to Evangelistic Association. The land is subject to a debt of $1.0 million, which the ministry would have to pay after taking the gift. However, the donor has said that she will not donate the land if the ministry has it appraised. The directors of Evangelistic Association decide to accept the donation and assume the $1.0 million debt under the conditions dictated by the donor. Should the directors of Evangelistic Association have accepted the donation subject to these terms?

A No. By not getting an appraisal, the directors of Evangelistic Association may have accepted a donation worth less than its assumed debt. Other assets of the ministry may now be at risk to satisfy the debt. Special tax rules for debt-financed property may make a sale of the land taxable to the ministry. Also, tax rules require an appraisal when gifts of land exceed a value of $5,000. Because the directors did not consider these factors and get a fair market appraisal, they breached their duty of care.

The duty of care means that directors should care about the organization they serve. Board decisions should be made deliberately out of a sense of deep concern for the best interests of the organization. It also means that directors should base their decisions upon facts and reliable information. The duty of care requires directors and officers not to act without first taking care to be properly informed.

The essence of a director's duty of care is to act under the circumstances with the care and concern of an ordinarily prudent person. This is the normal legal standard of director conduct. To act without having adequate information is to risk a foolish breach of the duty of care.

Q The pastor of City Church directed the church treasurer to pay $25,000 to a close friend of the pastor. This friend needed funds to pay a personal debt and avoid foreclosure on his house. The treasurer made the payment over protests, but neither he nor the pastor disclosed the matter to the church board. Yet the board of City Church did later learn of this improper transfer of funds. The board, however, did not take any action to collect the money or reprimand the pastor for using ministry assets to benefit a private individual. Did the board breach its duty of care?

A Yes. Directors are not liable for improper transactions that management hides from their knowledge. When the board discovers improper transactions, though, it has a duty to act. By failing to take any action after discovering this impropriety, the board breached its duty of care.

The duty of care is a duty to decide in the best interests of the organization. It is a duty that requires directors to be diligent in getting reliable information before deciding. It is a duty that advances and fulfills the corporation's religious purposes. To be careful, however, does not mean that directors must avoid making decisions that have a potential downside risk. Courts are not likely to second-guess a board's decision made prudently and in good faith. The potential for director liability is minimal when decisions are based on adequate investigation and are made in the best interests of the organization.

It is always possible that a board will make a poor decision, of course. Yet poor decisions are not necessarily an indication of a breach of the duty of care. So long as the decision is based upon facts and reliable opinions, the board has been diligent and has obeyed its duty of care. Board decisions are not held to a standard of perfection. Therefore, directors need not choose the best possible course of action as revealed by hindsight. Nor are directors required to act without emotion or the exercise of religious faith. They must, however, act in the light of relevant facts and information. In this way the board fulfills its duty of care.

The duty of loyalty

The duty of loyalty is closely related to a director's duty of care. The duty of loyalty requires directors to act in the best interests of the organization, not their own. It is a duty that embraces fairness, good faith, and honesty. It is the intention to advance and protect the organization free of any conflicts of interest or self-dealing. It requires directors to act without contemplating any direct or indirect personal financial gain or business opportunity.

Q The president of Parachurch, Inc. told the treasurer of a wholly owned profit subsidiary to pay $150,000 to a director of Parachurch, Inc. This was done so the director could make an overdue mortgage payment on some vacant land he owned. Before the payment was made, the director agreed to donate the land to Parachurch, Inc. Soon after the payment, he gave the land to the ministry free of all debt, which the board of Parachurch, Inc. accepted. However, neither the president nor the involved director told the board about the $150,000 payment. Was there a breach of the duty of loyalty?

A Yes. Both the president and the involved director breached their duties of loyalty by failing to disclose the nature of the transaction to the board. The value of the subsidiary stock held by Parachurch, Inc. was decreased by the amount of the payment. The director was unjustly enriched, not only by the cash he received, but also by the tax savings realized after donating the land. The director will be liable for taxes on the money he received and should not have voted to accept his donation. The payment was not in the best interests of either Parachurch, Inc. or its subsidiary.

In the above example nearly everything was mishandled. Neither the director nor the president disclosed the material facts of the transaction to the board of Parachurch, Inc. or its subsidiary. The payment of $150,000 to the director is an improper depletion of corporate assets. The payment personally enriched the director to the detriment of the subsidiary's creditors. The IRS could view the transaction as a fraudulent donation to a religious organization by a donor director.

The president's action shows that he did not respect the organizational distinctions between Parachurch, Inc. and its subsidiary. The president of one organization has no authority to direct the actions of an officer of a different corporation. His action is evidence that the subsidiary corporation is a mere *alter ego* of Parachurch, Inc. In other words, courts could view the subsidiary as a department of Parachurch, Inc., even though they are supposedly separate. If the subsidiary is found to be a mere alter ego, unpaid creditors of the subsidiary could seek collection from Parachurch, Inc. Such a finding would not be in the best interests of Parachurch, Inc.

The duty of obedience

The duty of obedience is a duty to carry out the organization's religious purposes and to obey the law. It requires a knowledge of the organization's mission and the laws that affect the carrying out of the mission. The duty of loyalty requires directors to take all necessary and reasonable measures to assure compliance with the law. This does not mean that directors are personally responsible for obeying every federal, state, and municipal law or regulation affecting the organization, however. Rather, directors are responsible to ensure that board policies and decisions obey the law. Management is responsible to ensure that its actions obey the law.

The discharge of this duty directly affects donors because it is the very thing they rely on when making gifts. Donors give to a religious organization for many reasons. But donor confidence largely depends on the belief that the organization is faithful to its mission. The mission of a religious organization is the reason it exists. This is an organization's most sacred trust. In a sense, the soul of a religious organization is its mission.

Ted Engstrom, president emeritus of World Vision, was asked to give his view of the importance of a religious organization's mission statement. He responded by saying,

> I think the mission statement is terribly important for any organization. It must be reviewed regularly by the chief officer to ensure that all programs line up with the mission statement. And furthermore, the board of directors should regularly review the mission statement and ask the question: Are we really fulfilling what we believe the mission of this organization to be?

In addition, donors implicitly assume that a religious organization is obeying the law. Religious organizations occupy a position of unique trust in our society. People expect ministries to be a shining example to the rest of society on how to behave. Donors expect secular institutions to cross the line of illegality on occasion, even if they do not approve of such conduct. On the other hand, donors never expect a ministry to which they donate to even come close to the line of illegality. Ministry insiders should keep the organization in full legal compliance. Therefore, the law expects that directors will fulfill their duty of obedience.

The Most Important Responsibility

Although the preceding duties are important, there are still other duties that may be more important. Their importance is not less merely because they are enforceable morally, not legally. Perhaps the single most important task of directors is to evaluate the performance of the organization's chief officer. In practice, directors of religious organizations rarely check the chief officer's performance. They are reluctant to do so for two reasons:

- The directors may have been appointed to or nominated for their positions by the chief officer.

- Directors may hesitate to check the performance of a person claiming a call from God to serve as the ministry head. The directors may believe that only God can hold the chief officer accountable.

Nevertheless, directors are legally and morally responsible to oversee organizational affairs. This responsibility includes evaluation of the chief officer. It even includes reprimanding the chief officer or terminating his or her employment if circumstances warrant. Such actions may seem extreme, but they are not. Directors are responsible to supervise the affairs of the organization and to act in its best interests. If a chief officer acts unethically or illegally, he or she should be confronted. It is not in the best interests of any ministry for improper conduct to go unchecked. If abuses are not curtailed when discovered, more abuses will occur. Soon the integrity of the entire organization will be compromised.

By checking his or her performance, the board demonstrates its power over the chief officer. Of course if the board does its job and selects the right person, it may never be faced with the unpleasant duty of confronting its chief officer. Chief officers should be selected at least in part for their administrative skills. The chief officer should also have the ability to attract and maintain generous donors and be skilled in carrying out the organization's mission. With the right person at the helm, the ministry sails much smoother.

Yet, power is best exercised with restraint. Perhaps the second most important task of the board is to support, encourage, and help the chief officer whenever possible—without meddling. A ministry can be accountable where boards and chief officers willingly and cooperatively share power in the best interests of the organization. Boards make and oversee policy, and chief officers execute policy while providing mission and challenge. Working together, directors and chief officers can fulfill their duties and advance the interests of the organizations they serve.

The duties described in this chapter are more than theoretical requirements. They are practical duties that can be carried out by every director. Directors and officers owe the organizations they serve undivided loyalty and a commitment to making the best possible decisions. Directors must carefully adhere to these duties and take their jobs seriously to set high standards of accountability. If they do so, the religious organizations they serve will grow stronger and be more effective in fulfilling their unique and needed mission.

5

Strengthening the Board of Directors

A BOARD OF DIRECTORS IS STRONG WHEN IT IS INDEPENDENT, involved, and informed. Such a board knows its role in governing an organization. A strong board not only establishes standards of accountability; it also creates a good environment for producing creative solutions to problems. Yet strong boards need strong directors. What kind of person makes a strong director?

Director Selection

■ **Don't pick the "yes" people (members and close friends of the family).**
Many organizations have boards primarily consisting of "yes" people who are unprepared as directors. "Yes" people are those who have a relationship with key ministry managers that will inhibit their holding management accountable. "Yes" people include the members and close friends of a key manager's family (or in-laws). These close friends may include the family pastor and

the family attorney. Occasionally, directors may be related to each other without being members or friends of a key manager's family, though this is less common and less of a problem for accountability purposes. Usually, when directors are related to each other, they are also related to a key manager.

There are two primary concerns with directors who are family members or close family friends of a key manager. First, "yes" people tend to be selected not because of what they *know* by way of experience or training, but because of who they *are* by way of relationship. This makes it likely that these "yes" people are not qualified decision makers and corporate overseers. Family members and friends of key managers often lack credibility and send a signal of weakness to donors and employees. Such family members and friends must work extra hard to rebut this presumption, if they can. The credibility problem is always difficult to overcome.

Second, and more important, "yes" people lack objectivity and independence even when they are otherwise qualified. Family members and friends cannot objectively address the issues confronting ministry management because of their relationships to the management. The interests of such directors are so intertwined with the interests of key managers that they have a conflict of interest when serving as a director. How can a director whose interests are linked to a key manager set high standards of accountability and be a check on management?

It is simply unfair to burden family members and family friends with organizational responsibilities as directors. They will obviously struggle with issues of objectivity when they need to be involved, ask questions, and demand necessary answers. Some ministry managers may understandably derive a sense of security and comfort from having family members and friends serving on their boards. Nonetheless, such directors will occasionally need to choose between calling management into account and preserving their good relationship. When that time comes, the relationship is almost always favored over accountability.

Picking "yes" people to serve as directors removes accountability from the organizational equation and produces ineffective board decisions. Left unattended and uncorrected, ineffective board decisions will weaken the organization. In turn, this will impede the effective carrying out of the organization's religious purposes and possibly bring about its demise.

This does not mean that members and close friends of a key manager's family are always unsuitable to serve as directors of the ministry. But these people, together with key managers, should never control the board. It is prudent to keep such persons to a minimum, perhaps no more than 20% of the total number of directors on the board. In this way, donors and others can tell that the organization is doing everything possible to maintain board independence, objectivity, and accountability. ECFA Standards of Responsible Stewardship (see Appendix F) require that the majority of directors of member organizations "not be employees/staff and/or related by blood or marriage."

Neither do we mean that all people who happen to be personal friends or acquaintances of key managers are to be shunned as possible directors. Friendly relationships between managers and directors are not the problem. A problem exists only when the director places the best interests of the manager above the best interests of the organization. Family members and close family friends, however, will be less likely to maintain their objectivity than other people. Credibility is hampered even when the director tries to be as objective as possible. Therefore wisdom suggests that these people not serve as directors, simply to avoid the appearance of impropriety.

▌ Don't select employees of the organization.
Employees who also serve as directors in the same organization are subject to some of the same concerns as family members and friends. Although employees will not be presumed to be unqualified, their objectivity and independence is still a problem.

Like family members, employees will have difficulty separating their personal interests from the organization's interests. Normally, only management level employees are selected for board membership. Yet these same people must hold management accountable for its actions. This is an obvious conflict of interest that negates accountability.

The Israelites were instructed in Deuteronomy 17 not to show contempt for any court order. The principle behind this is that no one can judge his or her own cause. That is, no one can hold himself or herself accountable—it must always be done by others; otherwise, justice is perverted. When people disobey a judge, they have placed their own self-judgment above the judgment of the court. In the same way, managers cannot be expected to act as directors and judge their own accountability. For them to do so is to judge their own cause, which is wrong.

Another problem faced by employee directors is the conflict that results when they must hold the chief officer accountable. If employees are called upon to judge or disclose certain misconduct of other managers, their jobs may be in jeopardy, especially if the managers under review have the power to fire them. No one likes to bite the hand that feeds him. If any manager holds the key to a director's job security, the director will be compromised in his or her ability to hold management accountable. Employee directors may serve the personal interests of the chief officer, but not the best interests of the organization.

A look at recognized standards in this area may be helpful. The Better Business Bureau standards for governance (Appendix C) state the following:

> Soliciting organizations shall have an independent governing board. Organizations whose directly and/or indirectly compensated board members constitute more than one-fifth (20%) of the total voting membership of the board or of the executive committee will not meet this standard.

There is a limited exception to the BBB standard for ordained clergy of a publicly soliciting church. Similarly, the Bylaws of the Ethics and Financial Integrity Commission (Appendix D) provide, "A majority of the Board of Directors shall be other than those joined by a family relationship, staff or employees." This standard does not apply to broadcast members with less than $100,000 in annual donation income from radio or television ministry, but it is a good idea in any event.

▍ Be careful about selecting the big financial contributor.

Just because someone is neither an employee of the ministry nor a family member of a key manager does not mean they will make a good director. One group of people organizations often select as directors are major donors to the ministry. What's wrong with selecting big financial contributors as directors? Nothing, if they understand the role of the board and are capable of making sound decisions. But there are few occasions when a lunch is truly free.

Donors are often viewed as the first source of directors by many religious organizations. Organizations that seek donors as directors may believe that: (1) the primary purpose of a board is to raise funds, (2) directors who are major donors will take personal ownership in one or more projects and keep the funds flowing, and (3) moneyed people are knowledgeable in the way organizations work and can make effective decisions. Nothing could be further from the truth.

First, the primary purpose of a board is to *govern*, not raise funds. The board will oversee all fund-raising programs of the organization, but it is not the job of a director to actually solicit funds. If a donor/director does actually raise funds, the organization may grow financially dependent upon his or her efforts or donations. It should not be assumed that because a prospective director has been a big contributor in the past, he or she will act the same in the future.

Nor is it wise to select directors solely because they might become major donors. Directors are the organization's overseers and their principal responsibilities are to make informed decisions in the best interests of the organization. Unless a major donor can also make positive nonfinancial contributions, his or her selection as a director could be a disaster. Any donations a prospective director might make are a low priority when it comes to evaluating qualifications.

Second, the big contributor may take ownership in the organization to an extreme position and seek to dictate policy. This is especially true when the director channels most of his or her donations to the ministry into a single project that he or she oversees. A feeling of ownership in this case will reduce objectivity when the merits of the project need to be reviewed. A feeling of ownership may also result in the director acting like an unofficial manager. This blurring of the distinction between the board and management only serves to diminish accountability.

Third, there is no correlation between having money and having training or experience. Wealthy people do not necessarily make better governors or decision makers. This does not mean that otherwise qualified persons should be rejected as directors merely because they are major donors. Still, it takes a whole lot more than financial standing to qualify as a competent director. Choose a director who is wealthy and competent, but do not assume one trait leads to the other.

■ **Do pick the "right stuff" (experience and expertise).**
In today's climate of increasing hostility toward religion, religious organizations must demonstrate their willingness to be account-able. The way to reach this goal is to have a strong board. A board of directors has extensive responsibilities. As the board does its job it creates an environment that will influence every director, employee, donor, and member. This influence will be either posi-

tive or negative in character. If negative, the organization will lose credibility and could eventually fail. If positive, the organization will gain credibility and have a better opportunity to prosper.

Understanding the true purpose of a governing board is the key to selecting good directors. Only good directors can make good board decisions. Good decisions energize the organization and move it toward fulfillment of its religious purposes. Some organizations consider the chief officer to be ordained to direct their affairs. The board is there only to support and confirm his or her vision or word from God. But such a view ignores the reality of the board's responsibilities. The board must direct the organization and hold management accountable for its actions.

Dr. Stephen E. Slocum, Jr., President of the American Tract Society, adds this insight on keeping the board energized:

> Another important part which I cannot emphasize too greatly is our rotation of the office of chairman. This office is filled by vote every year with a maximum of three (3) consecutive years. I find that this 3-year maximum is probably the single greatest factor in keeping our board alive and involved.

One of our survey questions asked managers to list the most important criteria for selecting the directors of a religious organization. The most comprehensive response was received from Bill Barta, executive assistant to the president of World Vision International. Mr. Barta concedes that World Vision had been wrestling with this question for years. One section of that organization's comprehensive criteria aptly demonstrates its commitment to picking the right stuff:

The general qualifications of directors:

- Spiritually mature, biblically literate, and active Christians

- Committed to WVI's objectives and philosophy

- Supportive of the president

- With an interest in international affairs

- With significant cross-cultural experience and sensitivity in addition to wide familiarity with their own country

- Able to work effectively in English

- Leaders in a sphere or profession

- Able to devote adequate time to WVI meetings, travel, and reading, in addition to their commitment to the Support Country Board, or to regional duties for members-at-large

- In control of their schedule so as to be able to regularly attend WVI Board and Committee meetings

- Able and ready to be advocates of WVI when opportunity presents itself

- Able to understand and use modern management practices.

Under these criteria, only persons who have requisite experience and expertise should be selected as directors. This is true even if they are unable to make significant financial contributions. These are the people who have the right stuff to assure donors that the religious organization they serve is accountable. Only people of this caliber can ensure that the organization intends to fulfill its religious purposes. Donors want and expect effective corporate governance that is accountable and capable. It is easy to select persons who are effective directors *if* the organization and its chief officer truly want effective, positive, and creative decisions.

Directors Are Guardians of Integrity

As mentioned earlier, directors are the guardians of organizational integrity. They are legally positioned in the organization to establish the highest possible standards of corporate accountability. The responses to our survey show that the chief officers of many ministries really want directors who will take a stand for accountability. They look for directors who are capable of making positive contributions (not necessarily monetary).

The following responses to our survey list some of the qualities of good directors and accountable boards:

- I perceive the necessary [director] criteria to be as follows: (1) spiritual integrity, (2) knowledge and support of the mission of the organization, (3) ability to give time, wealth, and influence commensurate with personal abilities, and (4) experience in responsible boardsmanship, especially in relationship to the non-profit sector.

    EDWARD L. HAYES, executive director of Mount Hermon

- I think [directors] must be alert to: (1) matters related to accountability, such as receipting, care, investment of money, (2) oversight of personnel with regard to personal Christian character and holiness of conduct, and (3) involvement in strategic planning to make the best use of the resources received in personnel and money.

    WADE T. COGGINS, executive director of the Evangelical Foreign Missions Association

- The board should provide organizational continuity and accept responsibility for its funding and financial accountability. It also needs to be well informed and to inform others continually.

    TED ENGSTROM, president emeritus of World Vision International

- The board has no higher responsibility than ensuring the integrity of the organization and that integrity must be embodied in the CEO.

    IAN M. HAY, general director of SIM International

- The board should be directly involved in the financial affairs of the organization, perhaps through a finance committee.

    RONALD A. BRETT, assistant director of TEAM

▌ Directors need four I's.

These responses show a widely shared appreciation for the character and skills of effective, positive, and contributing directors. Uniformly, respondents recognized that it takes effective directors to make an effective board. These responses may be summarized as four Is that every director needs to do his or her job: *Information, Integrity, Involvement,* and *Independence*.

Effective directors receive needed *information* for weighing the pros and cons of alternative courses of action and making proper decisions. Effective directors are men and women of *integrity* who govern the organization's business, financial, and ministry affairs. They are *involved* in board and board committee responsibilities and committed to the organization's mission. They are *independent* from management and exercise their oversight responsibilities objectively. Decisions are based upon facts and information free of conflicts of interest and the pressure of other directors or the chief officer.

■ **Directors must be willing to root out problems.**

Directors must be willing to identify problems in ministry management and root them out. One of the problems that affects many religious organizations is their increased activism in partisan politics. The Internal Revenue Code specifically prohibits tax-exempt religious organizations from engaging in partisan politics. Yet some religious organizations openly engage in political campaigns, using tax-exempt funds for this prohibited purpose while their boards sit idly by.

> **Q** During the last Congressional campaign two employees of Media Ministry stopped automobiles that were exiting the ministry parking lot. They passed out campaign literature and encouraged other employees to attend a political rally in behalf of a particular candidate. Media Ministry permitted this activity and openly endorsed the candidate, a Christian, in his bid for election. Management personnel perceived this as merely putting their faith into practice. What is the board's responsibility if it learns of this situation?

> **A** The board should act quickly to stop all political campaigning activity on corporate premises. It should also take steps to ensure that management stops making any further political endorsements. Political activity by exempt religious organizations is specifically prohibited by U.S. tax laws. If discovered by the IRS, this activity will jeopardize Media Ministry's tax-exempt status, which the board must act to protect.

The political activism of some prominent religious leaders has increased, especially during the past two presidential election campaigns. Like it or not, the law prohibits religious organizations from engaging, even a little bit, in partisan politics. In addition, such activities are offensive to many Americans who question the use of tax-exempt funds of religious organizations for partisan politics. This is the kind of problem a board needs to know about and be willing to root out when discovered.

Matters that beset almost all organizations include employee morale and personnel problems. These problems, if left unattended, spread like a cancer throughout an organization and adversely affect employee turnover and productivity. For instance, religious organizations tend to underpay their employees and extend few fringe benefits. Their employee compensation compares unfavorably with similarly situated and qualified employees in business and even government.

Religious organizations apparently believe their employees are content to live on a lesser salary merely because they serve in a ministry capacity. This logic, however, does not make sense. Food, clothing, and shelter cost as much for employees of religious organizations as they cost for employees of government and businesses. Religious organizations can and should do better. At the very least they should pay competitive wages and benefits to their employees.

The constant problem of changing conditions and circumstances affects every religious organization. Successful religious organizations confront their problems and solve them rather than hide their heads in the sand. An involved board will take seriously its duty to identify problems and root them out. A strong board will make effective decisions that solve problems and keep the organization moving forward.

▎ Directors must work with management.

The relationship between the board and management should be objective, but not adversarial. It should be independent, yet supportive, open and without deception. The board and management comprise a team that should work cooperatively toward fulfilling the organization's religious purposes. This is the primary goal of the organization and every reasonable effort should be expended to achieve it.

Nevertheless, the board and management each have their respective organizational powers. In many religious organizations a domineering or charismatic chief officer can easily intimidate a volunteer board and assume virtually all organizational power. If this happens, the risk is high that few restraints will be imposed upon the chief officer. Eventually organizational accountability flies out the window, and anything can happen.

Conversely, if the board assumes virtually all organizational power, it risks making the chief officer ineffective. The chief officer then loses the ability to provide the organization with vision and effective administration. What is needed, of course, is a proper balance between the board and management. The board and the chief officer must each operate within their respective spheres of authority and power. Each should respect the other, and both should be pulling the organization in the same positive direction.

Dr. Slocum, of the American Tract Society, clearly understands the nature of this sensitive balance of power. He says,

> our responsibility is to communicate facts to our constituency. This is done by frequent references to our board members in letters and publications sent to our members and friends, as well as listing them where practical in our publications. I make a point of letting the members and friends know that I am responsible to a board in the final analysis, and am not a king over a ministry that is built around a personality.

Of course, it is possible for the balance of power to be skewed in either direction. That is, either the board or the chief officer may take control away from the other. It is better for the sake of the organization, however, that the power be shared between the board and its chief officer to promote harmony and accountability.

▼

Every ministry needs to bring about a constructive sharing of power between its board and chief officer to set the standard of accountability. An organization might consider implementing as many of the following ten accountability steps as are applicable:

☐ Amend the bylaws to permit the chief officer to have broad executive authority within the scope of the organization's religious purposes.

☐ Authorize membership in the Evangelical Council for Financial Accountability (ECFA), the Ethics and Financial Integrity Commission (EFICOM) or any comparable financial accountability organization.

☐ Adopt a comprehensive ethics and conflict-of-interest policy applicable to all officers, directors, and employees.

☐ Approve a detailed annual operating budget, an annual independent financial audit, and an annual mission compliance review.

☐ Authorize and monitor general and specific fund solicitation programs in compliance with the Council of Better Business Bureaus' Standards for Charitable Solicitations and ECFA, EFICOM, or equivalent standards.

☐ Adopt a policy and compliance procedure to avoid substantial unrelated business income or lobbying activities and any involvement in partisan politics.

☐ Approve an annually prepared three-year business and ministry plan including cash flow and income projections.

☐ Authorize and empower appropriate working management committees including audit, development, executive, finance, and nominating committees of the board.

☐ Approve procedures for the selection and performance evaluation of executive and operating officers and hold them accountable for appropriate execution of board policies.

☐ Make informed policy decisions consistent with and supportive of the organization's exempt religious purpose and tax-exemption laws free of conflicts of interest and self-dealing.

▲

█ Directors who do their job can breathe easily about exposure to liability.

Directors can relax about being sued when they do their job. It is true that courts stagger under the weight of shareholder suits against directors of business corporations. But there are few reported instances of such suits against directors of nonprofit organizations. For example, we are not aware of a single lawsuit for breach of duty against a director or an officer of a religious organization in California. Some suits are known to have been filed, settled, and later dismissed in other states, though.

Reported breach-of-duty suits against nonprofit directors are rare for two reasons. First, few people have the right (or standing) to sue a nonprofit director. Second, there is little incentive for those having standing (usually corporate insiders) to sue fellow directors or officers. At the present time, those who can sue directors and officers are limited to the organization itself, insiders (including directors) and members-at-large in membership organizations. Still, directors and officers who are careful to do their jobs will avoid liability for any actions taken or omitted.

At present, donors cannot sue directors and officers of a religious organizations for general mismanagement. Nor is it likely they will soon have this standing. Some argue that donors resemble stockholders of business corporations and should therefore be entitled to sue directors and officers for alleged breach of duties. This argument is based on the belief that donors have rights of ownership in a nonprofit organization similar to stockholders. But this belief is without merit, as discussed in Chapter 2. Donors have no general right to sue because in most cases they have suffered no losses that can be recovered.

Nonetheless donors in some states do have a limited right to sue organizations for solicitation fraud or a diversion of assets. These specific claims against religious organizations will be examined in a later chapter.

The remaining principal area of concern for directors relates to lawsuits brought by persons claiming personal injuries or property damage. These suits, called *third party suits,* are brought primarily against the organization itself. Directors and officers may occasionally be included as defendants in the hope of getting a speedy settlement.

Because a nonprofit corporation has a separate and distinct legal identity, it must pay or satisfy its own debts and obligations. The key to avoiding or successfully defending third party suits is for directors and officers to responsibly fulfill their duties. So long as this is done, they are not likely to be sued. If they are sued, they will likely prevail. Still, directors and officers should discuss their potential liability with a qualified insurance broker or agent who can recommend insurance coverage.

The Ability to Take Effective Action

A strong board consists of informed, involved, and independent directors who act with a deep sense of integrity. They are committed to the organization's mission and are aware of their duties. Each director knows that he or she must act with care, loyalty, and obedience. The organization and its members expect the board to fulfill these duties and good directors take these duties seriously.

Yet it is not a one-way street. Organizations have reciprocal duties to the board that must be exercised with integrity. These duties must also be taken seriously. The extent to which these duties are fulfilled will determine how well the board can do its job. Even though the board sits at the top of the organizational hierarchy, its role can be thwarted. Therefore, the organization has a duty not to impede the normal operation of the board, by such conditions as:

An inactive board of directors
Directors cannot discharge their duties on behalf of an organization unless they meet regularly. Practices vary among religious organizations, but boards must meet often enough to make policy, oversee management, and set high standards of accountability. Normally, three or four board meetings per year is appropriate. On occasion, special emergency meetings may need to be called. If management or certain directors refuse to schedule regular board meetings, it can seriously impede the effectiveness of the board. A board that meets once each year or less is really an inactive board, ill-prepared to fulfill its duties.

The Council of Better Business Bureaus, Inc. clearly recognizes the need for a charitable organization to have an active governing body. Paragraph 2 of its section on governance in the Standards for Charitable Solicitation (Appendix C) states,

An active governing body (board) exercises responsibility in establishing policies, retaining qualified executive leadership, and overseeing that leadership.

An active board meets formally at least three times annually, with meetings evenly spaced over the course of the year, and with a majority of the members in attendance (in person or by proxy) on average.

Because the public reasonably expects board members to participate personally in policy decisions, the governing body is not active, and a roster of board members may be misleading, if a majority of the board members attend no formal board meetings in person over the course of a year.

If the full board meets only once annually, there shall be at least two additional, evenly spaced meetings during the year of an executive committee of board members having interim policy-making authority, with a majority of its members present in person, on average.

Virtually identical criteria are adopted as part of the EFICOM Bylaws (Appendix D) for members of that broadcasting organization. ECFA Standards of Responsible Stewardship (Appendix F) specify that boards of member organizations shall meet at least semi-annually.

These standards say it all. Any organization that fails to meet these minimal standards cannot discharge its duty to the board. The organization can easily remove impediments to effective board action by scheduling regular board meetings. There is no excuse for the lack of regular meetings.

A lack of full disclosure

The daily operations of any organization are handled by management, not the board. Letters, notices, and inquiries do not come addressed to directors, but to managers. Thus directors have little opportunity to find out what is going on in an organization apart from what management discloses to them. Boards rely on management disclosures of ministry and business affairs. They make decisions and govern the organization primarily on the basis of these same disclosures. Although directors have a duty to ask questions and sometimes even probe for answers, management has a corresponding duty to disclose matters to the board.

The reciprocal duties owed between the board and management enhance an organization's accountability. When the board and management fulfill their roles, it shows that each respects the power of the other in their respective spheres of authority. Management's duty to disclose is discussed at length in Chapter 7, but there is an application in the present context. Management must disclose to the board certain unusual items or else the board cannot do its job effectively. In our opinion, the following kinds of information should always be disclosed to the full board as soon as opportunity permits:

- Favored status of certain employees, expectations by certain employees of nonstandard perquisites or benefits, and any unusual employee relationships with the organization outside the normal course of business

- Changes in strategic planning that affect the organization's capacity to fulfill its mission

- Threats of violence against the organization, any of its employees, or against anyone in the custody or control of the organization

- Suspected illegal or criminal acts of any employee while acting in the scope of employment (this includes the payment or acceptance of kickbacks or inducements in connection with any vendor to the organization)

- Understandings, whether verbal or written, related to management succession

- Litigation threatened or pending against an individual officer or director arising out of any conduct in his or her capacity as such.

When effectiveness is impeded

There may be times when a board will be faced with the inability to take effective action. There may be an unwillingness to schedule regular board meetings. Or meetings are scheduled, but management is ill-prepared and some directors never show. Perhaps management is reluctant to make a disclosure of important matters that are discovered only when it is too late. What should a director do who is caught in a situation like this? What action would a strong director consider at this point?

First, encourage those people in the organization who may, perhaps unwittingly, be impeding the effective operation of the board. People may simply be unaware of what things are expected of them in their official capacity. Take time aside from a formal meeting to explain what might be done to increase the board's effectiveness. Offer to help initiate new procedures for board meetings, if appropriate. Whether everyone knows exactly how to act in the organization is not as important as their willingness to learn.

Second, if someone in management is responsible for intentionally impeding the board, the board should take action to hold that manager accountable. The first thing to do is suggest how the manager can improve his or her performance. If a manager does not respond to correction, dismissal and replacement may be appropriate. Unless a board is willing to take this step when needed, it can never truly hold management accountable for its actions.

Third, if the full board fails to take corrective action when needed, a conscientious director must be prepared to resign. This assumes the board has already been fully advised as to what the problem is and what can be done about it. A strong board consists of strong individual directors. A strong director is one who will act on the basis of principled integrity to protect the best interests of the organization. When that is no longer possible, he or she should consider resigning to avoid personal liability for board inaction.

As 1 Timothy 3:1-2 reminds us, "If anyone sets his heart on being an overseer, he desires a noble task. Now the overseer must be above reproach . . . ."

6

Ten Tips for a Smooth Board Meeting

Is YOUR BOARD OF DIRECTORS OR TRUSTEES AN EFFECTIVE WORKING body? Or does it get stuck in meetings with endless reports and aimless discussions without taking any real action? Consider these ten practical tips on how to run a smooth board meeting and increase the board's effectiveness.

■ **Don't expect the board of directors to act as a management committee.**
It is not the job of the board to do the work management should do. One of the biggest problems faced by many governing boards is the temptation to act as a management committee. Management committees examine alternatives, undertake studies, review reports, and propose programs for board approval. Committees prepare and shape policy issues for presentation to the board. They do the fact-finding, but boards decide. In summary, committees are a tool of management, not the board. When a board acts as a

management committee the result is reduced accountability, even in smaller organizations. Accountability is reduced because the committee approach blurs the distinction between management and the board. It is hard for the board to hold management accountable when the board performs management tasks itself.

Even for policy matters properly coming before the board, it is not the role of the directors to propose plans of action, research the merits of each proposal, and decide how to proceed. It is the job of managers or a management committee to do all of this before the board meeting. Management should then propose a single plan of action for the board to accept or reject. Management should make available its research and findings so directors may ask questions, but the board should not actually do this work itself.

▋ Prepare all board resolutions in advance of the meeting.

One of the best ways to avoid the committee problem is to prepare all proposed board resolutions in advance of the meeting. This will save time during the meeting when one person tries to figure out how to word something while everyone else waits. Worse yet, every director may want to help draft each resolution. It is better to draft proposed resolutions in a relaxed atmosphere when all relevant factors can be carefully weighed. It is more difficult to try to come up with all the right words under pressure in front of the board.

In addition, individual scheduling conflicts and other factors make meeting time very precious. It is better for management to take two hours drafting proposed resolutions in advance than to take fifteen minutes of discussion time away from the board. Of course, resolutions occasionally need to be drafted during a meeting, such as when an item not on the agenda is brought up for discussion. But this should be the exception rather than the rule. It is also best not to defer all resolution drafting until after the meeting. When this is done it raises questions about what the board really said.

■ **Send each director an information packet two weeks before the meeting.**

To assist the board, management should send all pre-drafted proposed resolutions to the directors two weeks before the meeting. An agenda and all supporting paperwork should accompany the proposed resolutions. This enables the directors to see the full scope of what management intends to cover during the meeting, and to think about each issue in advance. Each director knows, before going into the meeting, exactly what action management is proposing the board take.

When the meeting begins, each director will already have an idea of where the discussion of each agenda item should go. He or she does not need to waste time finding out what management wants to do. If the treasurer gives a report, directors should not have to waste time looking at financial statements for the first time, searching for key information. The statements should have been included in the information packet sent earlier. During the meeting the directors can focus their attention on taking action, which is what meetings are for, rather than engaging in mere fact-finding.

■ **Meet at least three times each year.**

It is extremely rare for a board of directors to meet too often. Usually boards do not meet often enough. Sometimes directors may not realize what it is they need to do, so there is not much point in meeting frequently—so they think. Alternatively, management may not be aware of things they need to bring to the board's attention. There is nothing worse than a board that meets only once annually to say hello, approve the reports of the president and treasurer, and then say good-bye. Such a board can hardly hold management accountable for anything.

There is no such thing as honorary board positions. Every director is a working member of the organization, and needs to get involved in a review of operations on a regular basis. If management is not bringing organizational matters to the board's attention regularly, the directors need to go looking for them. Standard practice requires a board to meet three times each year, or once each year with two executive committee meetings of the board in between. See the Better Business Bureau Standards for Charitable Solicitations (Appendix C) and the EFICOM Membership Criteria (Appendix D). The plain truth is that a board that meets only once each year is not taking its role seriously enough.

▌ **Telephonic board meetings should be the exception, not the rule.**

To do its job well, any board needs to be thorough. Directors need time to read over documents, assess them, and discuss matters among themselves. They also need access to management personnel to answer questions and produce additional documents or give reports if requested. A conference call, though convenient, works against thoroughness. Discussion is difficult to lead and interaction is limited. Further, it is difficult to hold a telephonic meeting for several hours, as board meetings often require. As a result, telephonic meetings tend to make directors less effective in discharging their oversight responsibilities and in holding management accountable for its actions.

Of course, telephonic meetings are sometimes useful and proper. When the board needs to act quickly, a telephonic meeting is a big help. Yet a board should do this only when it needs to act before it can hold the next regular meeting. This would be a device of convenience particularly suited for use in an emergency. There is no reason to conduct a regular meeting as though it were an emergency. This defeats the ability of the board to investigate carefully and deliberate about matters brought before it.

▌ **Don't hold meetings in different vacation spots.**

Planning a board meeting within a vacation setting is like shaking oil and water together—they do not blend well for long. Sooner or later they separate, and the vacation always comes out on top.

There is no greater hindrance to being thorough than a scheduled vacation activity in the middle of the day. The purpose of a board meeting is serious business, not pleasure, and the atmosphere of the meeting should enhance getting work done. Board meetings do not have to be boring, but why go out of the way to short-circuit thoroughness? A board focused on pleasure cannot also focus itself on accountability.

There is nothing wrong with meeting in a resort area if that is where the organization has its headquarters. Nor is it wrong if it is the best mid-point place for all directors. But to go looking for different resort areas in which to hold meetings misses the point of holding meetings in the first place. Board meetings are not an excuse for organization insiders to take their spouses on a vacation tax free. The job of a director is too important to interfere with it in this way. Take the directors on a vacation between meetings, not during them.

▌ **It is better to preserve dissenting votes than unanimity.**
Among many religious organizations there is a myth that the organization is best served by unanimity among the leadership in all matters. This concept is often based upon the principle that strength comes from unity. Unanimity, however, is only important in matters that are themselves essential to the organization. As the adage goes, "In essentials unity, in non-essentials liberty, and in all things charity." Since matters coming before the directors normally require only a majority vote for approval, it is the spirit of liberty (to disagree) that should prevail. The charter or bylaws will specify matters that require unanimity.

One of the keys to holding management accountable is free and open discussion among directors. This is likely to produce dissenting votes from time to time. Conversely, the lack of any dissent betrays the probable lack of free and open discussion. From a liability perspective, the more essential an issue is to the organization, the more crucial dissent becomes to each director. If the board is held liable for its decisions, only directors who preserve their dissents for the record can relieve themselves from liability. Concern for both liability and accountability demands that directors have freedom to dissent from time to time.

▌ Discourage voting abstentions except when a conflict of interest exists.

Directors may sometimes wish to abstain from voting on a resolution rather than to vote against it. This action is often a response to the pressure to exhibit unanimity among the directors. Some perceive abstention as an inoffensive way to note an objection while leaving the unanimity intact. Though such conduct may please management, it does not serve the best interests of the organization. When regularly practiced, abstention produces a "rubber stamp approval" type of board of directors that cannot hope to hold management accountable for its actions.

Abstention is only appropriate for a director when asked to vote on a matter in which he or she has a personal conflict of interest. A conflict of interest exists when a director's loyalties are divided, especially when corporate action may result in personal gain. Apart from conflict-of-interest situations, abstention is merely a spineless way for a director to object. And, from a liability perspective, abstentions by directors present at a meeting will count the same as a vote of approval. A director must actually record a dissenting vote to avoid responsibility in a matter the board has approved.

▌ Don't take lengthy minutes of reports or discussions during a meeting.

Taking minutes of a board meeting is something of an art. Management needs to know what matters to bring to the board's attention and what kind of action is appropriate. It takes practice to know how to word resolutions and what to include in the minutes. Occasionally, people go overboard in making a full report of board discussions when drafting the minutes. They include every last detail of who said what, when, and in reply to whom, during a meeting. Board discussions do not need to be shown in the minutes at all. Of all that the directors say in each matter, only the final resolution is important.

Minutes should handle management reports a bit differently. The purpose of a management report is not to spend time telling ministry stories. Nor is its purpose to sell the board on the positive aspects of the organization and its ministry. Its purpose is to inform the board of material facts that directors need in order to take proper action. Some brief record of the report may be useful to state what facts were before the board when it made its decision. This protects both management and the board should liability for the decision become an issue. It is enough to summarize the key points of a report or to include a separate document by reference.

▌ Don't take any minutes of prayers, devotions, or Bible studies.
For similar reasons, board meeting minutes do not need to report prayers, devotions, and Bible studies. Certainly devotions have a legitimate place at board meetings, but not to the point where they become the focus of the gathering. It is enough to note that someone opened the meeting with prayer and led the board in a short devotional before proceeding with its business. Any recitation of who read which verse, what was prayed for, or what spiritual insight was gained is totally extraneous.

Even though the board may preside over a religious organization, its primary role is not to discuss religious insights. Its task is to direct the affairs of the organization that have any legal, financial, business, or strategic impact. Maintaining doctrinal purity may be a valid concern for the board, but only as a business item on the agenda that requires some action. The board should not spend an excessive amount of time concerning itself with religious matters that are not formal business items. Such action betrays a lack of understanding about what it is a board should do.

7
Managing with Integrity

WHAT DOES IT MEAN TO MANAGE A RELIGIOUS ORGANIZATION WITH integrity? According to Ted Engstrom, "Integrity has to do with lifestyle, with the way we treat our employees, with telling the truth no matter what the results may be. Integrity is forthright, it has the other person's well-being in mind, it means that you'll keep your promises." But few organizations keep their promises all the time; still fewer, whether religious or otherwise, operate from the perspective of doing what's right in every situation.

A religious organization should distinguish itself from all other organizations by doing what is right. To manage a religious organization with integrity means to do what is right. Its management knows its responsibilities and carries them out with enthusiasm. Managers know the limits of their authority and act accordingly, weighing ethical concerns before making decisions.

The general tasks of management include planning, organizing, staffing, directing, inspiring, and leading other people. Managers take the resources available to them, such as people, finances, information, equipment, and materials, and orchestrate them to accomplish the ministry's purposes. This is true whether the manager is the chief executive officer or at any other level of management within the organization. The challenge of managers is to do their job both effectively and with integrity. The process of management begins by knowing management's responsibilities.

Management's Responsibilities

The management of a religious organization demands the cooperative efforts of boards and management. Without visionary leaders, many influential ministries would not exist. As organizations grow in size and complexity, the need for a management team becomes increasingly necessary.

But few individuals have all of the skills needed to manage complex organizations. Not only does management require competence in effective ministry, it also requires competence in business. Many ministries, like some professionals, resist acknowledging that they are "in business" because it sounds too commercial. But most ministries inevitably confront business challenges similar to what business organizations encounter. Therefore, ministry managers, like business managers, are accountable for their actions in many ways. Let's look at a few of them.

Management is accountable to the board

Management is accountable to the board of directors as a matter of legal responsibility. Since the board of directors appoints all corporate officers and all ministry managers report to those officers, management as a whole is accountable to the board.

For what is it accountable? Managers are accountable for how they fulfill their duties. In general, responsible managers must act efficiently and with integrity.

Management also is responsible to follow recognized standards of conduct. Because managers are agents of the organization, they are subject to agency rules—they are responsible to act honestly, in good faith, and to deal fairly with the organization. One widely accepted set of standards of conduct for corporate officers is from the 1986 Revised Model Nonprofit Corporation Act (see Appendix B). These standards of conduct are not law in every state, but they have been applied to businesses in many states. Courts are likely to apply these standards to managers of religious organizations as well.

These standards require officers with discretionary authority to act in good faith, with the care of an ordinarily prudent person, and in the best interests of the organization. When accepting a position as a manager, a person implicitly agrees to act in the best interests of the organization. He or she agrees to exercise good faith in all transactions and to act within the scope of his or her authority. If a manager has a conflicting personal interest in a transaction, it must yield to the best interests of the organization.

Q A brother of the executive pastor of City Church owns a construction company. A recent earthquake damaged a classroom building owned by City Church. Without consulting the board of trustees, the executive pastor signed a noncompetitive bid with his brother's company to make the repairs. The trustees were unaware that the pastor's brother owned the construction firm until City Church complained about the quality of the repairs. Did the executive pastor act in the best interests of City Church?

A No. The pastor acted in the best interests of his brother, not City Church. He failed to get competitive bids and find the best contractor available for the job. He did not follow recognized standards of conduct and is accountable to the church board for his actions.

Being accountable to a board means more than fulfilling one's legal responsibilities. It means that responsibilities will be carried out competently with enthusiasm and integrity. For example, in 2 Corinthians 8, the apostle Paul discusses the administration of funds collected from the church at Corinth, located about 50 miles west of Athens, Greece. Paul was entrusted to carry these funds to Jerusalem in Israel for distribution to the poor. The scope of his management authority was limited. Any deviation from his appointed task would have violated the scope of his authority.

Paul clearly understood he was accountable to the Corinthian church for the proper management of the funds. He said, "For we are taking pains to do what is right, not only in the eyes of the Lord but also in the eyes of men" (verse 21). This is the admonition to all ministry managers: *Do what is right, not only in the eyes of the Lord but also in the eyes of people.*

Today donors want to know whether the managers of religious organizations are capable and financially responsible. Donors ask whether management is accountable to a board and whether the board understands its responsibilities to govern. In short, donors want some assurance that management acts with integrity. These are difficult but legitimate questions that ministries must answer—for at least two reasons. First, management and the board owe donors accomplishment, commitment, effectiveness, integrity, and priority. Second, donors have a right to know whether they support a financially responsible and accountable organization managed by competent people.

Increased business challenges, especially financial and legal challenges, require managers to be more active in their administrative roles. They must do so if they hope to avoid public criticism and possible personal liability. If managers fail to act responsibly and decisively, religious organizations are in for trouble. Congress will likely seek expansion of IRS powers of inquiry through simpler church audit procedures and increased financial disclosure requirements. Courts may also get into the act by giving donors standing to sue religious organizations and their managements for breaches of duty.

Management must keep within its discretionary authority

Q The administrator of Christian School is also the corporate treasurer. The bylaws give the treasurer the power to make loans to students in aggregate amounts less than $5,000. The administrator has made a practice of using school funds to make loans averaging $2,000 each to faculty members, his sister, and himself. None of the borrowers is a student at Christian School. The board of regents has just learned of this practice and wants to know what it can do. Has the administrator acted within the scope of his authority?

A No. A manager or officer has no recognized power to make loans unless specifically authorized to do so. Here, the manager's authority is limited to student loans. He has discretion in choosing loan applicants and amounts. He does not have discretion to make loans to nonstudents. The administrator is accountable to the board for his actions.

As discussed earlier, the role of directors is to establish policy and to oversee and hold management accountable for its actions. Management, on the other hand, is responsible to manage daily operations. This means that the board defines the limits of management authority. Beyond these limits a manager must not go, or else he or she has violated the trust of the board. To exceed these limits is to act contrary to the best interests of the organization. Within

these limits, however, managers have *discretionary authority*—
they can choose the best way to accomplish any task within their
authority as they see fit.

Management's discretionary authority is obviously limited to
the purposes stated in the organization's bylaws or board resolutions. Any change in these purposes must come from the board or
the organization's voting members. Managers sometimes dismiss
bylaws and board resolutions because, in their view, these formalities or technicalities restrict their effectiveness. But the limits
of management's authority specified by the bylaws and board
resolutions are the primary standards of management integrity and
accountability.

Management must handle its responsibilities within the limits
of its discretionary authority, because every manager is an *agent*
(a person who acts for someone else, called the *principal)* under
specific instructions. An agent's instructions set forth what his or
her responsibilities are and define the limits of his or her authority.
While management is accountable to the board, its accountability
can be checked only as the board defines management's authority
to act. The board does this by adopting resolutions or by reference
to a bylaw provision.

The bylaws of a religious organization will typically define the
authority and duties of its president, secretary, and treasurer in
these terms:

☐ The president is the chief executive officer of the corporation
   subject to the control of the board. The president may begin,
   direct, supervise, and control the organization's various ministries. He or she presides at all meetings of the board of directors
   and of the members. The president is an unofficial member of
   all standing committees. The president has authority to exercise
   all voting rights of stocks or bonds the organization may hold.

☐ The secretary keeps the corporate seal and all minute books of the meetings of directors and members. He or she also keeps the membership records. The secretary gives any required notices of the meetings of the board of directors or the members. The secretary shall perform other duties as required by law, the board of directors, or the bylaws.

☐ The treasurer is the chief financial officer of the corporation. He or she keeps the financial records and books of the corporation according to recognized accounting practices. The treasurer may make sure an annual audit is prepared each fiscal year by licensed public accountants. He or she is also responsible to prepare periodic financial statements for the board to review.

☐ Each of these officers usually has other powers and duties that the board or the bylaws may define, as well as powers most corporate officers in similar positions are expected to have. In addition, the bylaws may provide for other officers, such as a number of vice presidents. The duties of each of these should be thought out with care and tailored to each organization. Standard bylaw forms can be bought in any office supply store, but tailor them to suit your specific needs.

It is right for managers to expect the board expressly to delegate administrative powers to management. The board must delegate enough power to permit an effective administration of daily operations. Yet it cannot delegate power too broadly or accountability cannot be maintained. The powers of management must be stated clearly, without being unduly restrictive. The board may confer broad powers in some areas and narrow powers in other areas. The overall purpose is to make management effective and accountable at the same time.

Again, this does not mean that management may only take those actions that the charter and bylaws expressly spell out. This would unduly restrict management and make it ineffective in carrying out its responsibilities. Management has the right to exercise discretion in choosing the means used to fulfill the purposes expressed in the charter and bylaws. Management, though restricted in the scope of its activities, can be innovative in carrying out these activities.

Management has implied authority to act

Q The executive director of Missions Board gave two acres of ministry land to a missionary friend who promptly built a home on it. The executive director did not disclose this matter to the board for prior approval or later ratification. The executive director believed he had authority to deal with ministry assets as he thought best. Can the directors of Missions Board set aside the transfer of land?

A No. The executive director clearly showed a lack of understanding of his discretionary authority. Still, the only question for the missionary is whether it was reasonable for him to rely on the apparent authority of the executive director. If this belief was reasonable, the directors cannot set aside the transfer. The missionary probably did have a reasonable belief because the executive director held himself out as having unlimited discretion when acting for the organization.

In some religious organizations management exercises almost unlimited authority to run the organization as it sees fit on a daily basis. No one makes the distinction between purposes and means, so managers make basic purpose-type decisions on their own.

Because of limited resources, they may conclude that they have little choice but to act quickly. Yet, when this happens, they have retreated from accountability. The solution is not for management to blame the bylaws, an incompetent board, or cumbersome board resolutions. Rather, management should propose shaping the bylaws to meet organizational needs, look for competent directors, and seek authority to carry out desired purposes. Management must work these things out with the board.

There are some differences between an organization and the rest of the world, however. Other people can hold an organization liable for the actions of managers even when such actions exceed their authority. This is a result of the law of *implied authority*. Implied authority arises when the organization leads people to believe that managers have authority to act for the ministry even though they lack actual authority. But it is not the responsibility of vendors to determine whether managers are acting within their authority—it is the organization's responsibility.

This happens frequently in organizations lacking effective accountability procedures. When someone holds an organization liable for management's actions on the basis of implied authority, there is little to commend it as an accountable organization. What management and the boards of some religious organizations often ignore is that management's authority is not unlimited.

Management must disclose matters of significance

Q The personnel director of Parachurch, Inc. routinely makes policy decisions affecting the wages, hours, or working conditions of all ministry employees. She carries out her policies without the benefit of board approval. Her policy decisions are careful, made in good faith, and almost always in the best interests of the organization. Is

the personnel director acting within the scope of her
discretionary authority?

A No. Policy decisions are the responsibility of the board.
The personnel director's role is to make recommendations to the board and to provide the board with information and facts. By setting policies affecting the
wages, hours, and working conditions of Parachurch,
Inc. employees, the personnel director exceeded her
authority.

Because management is responsible to act within the limits of its
authority, it must disclose all matters of significance to the board.
The board can make policy only as it has knowledge of all matters
that may significantly affect its policy decisions. Yet, the board is
not interested in insignificant matters clearly within management's
discretionary authority to handle. Sometimes it's difficult to know
which matters require disclosure to the board and which matters
fall within management's authority to handle. How can management know when to disclose a matter to the board?

The test for knowing when to disclose a matter to the board is
simply stated: *If the matter is routine and falls within the scope of
management's discretionary authority, it need not be disclosed to
the board. Management should disclose matters falling outside the
scope of its discretionary authority that significantly affect organizational interests.*

▼

The following list is not exhaustive, but it illustrates matters that
usually fall outside the scope of management's discretionary
authority. These items should normally be disclosed as a matter
of integrity to the board of directors before management takes
action if at all possible:

☐ actual and threatened litigation

☐ joint venture and partnership arrangements

☐ contractual matters outside the normal and usual course of business

☐ entering into any government contract

☐ fund solicitation program changes

☐ changes in the chain of command

☐ formation of subsidiary and affiliate organizations

☐ dissolution of subsidiary and affiliate organizations

☐ loans proposed to be made or borrowed

☐ plans materially affecting the financial condition of the organization

☐ notice of tax audit or other government agency review of the organization

☐ suspected illegal conduct by any employee or agent

☐ adoption or change of any employee benefit plans

☐ starting or stopping an area of the organization's operations

☐ submitting applications to any government agency.

▲

A Measure of Management's Integrity

Organizational accountability

An important measure of management's integrity is its commitment to the organization's mission. The word *mission* describes the organization's strategy for accomplishing its religious purposes. The heart of a religious organization is its mission, and nothing should be allowed to interfere with its accomplishment. Whenever an organization strays from its mission, it loses its effectiveness.

An organization fulfills its mission by focusing upon it with great intensity. It's similar to someone hitting a ball with a bat. The only way the person will hit the ball is if the person focuses only upon the ball. Everything else is ignored and every ounce of energy is committed to hitting the ball. So it is with an organization's mission. Unless management ignores everything else and commits every resource to fulfilling the organization's mission, the mission will never be fulfilled. The only way to fulfill the mission is to focus everything upon it and not to let it out of sight.

Management is responsible to communicate, explain, and defend the organization's mission to its donors and employees. Not only will regular communication keep the vision alive, it will keep the organization alive. For a religious organization to remain vibrant, its mission must beat steadily to circulate life-giving energy throughout the entire ministry. There is no other reason for a religious organization to exist but for the accomplishment of its mission. This is what sets it apart from all other organizations. This is why donors give to religious organizations.

Managers of religious organizations sometimes pursue opportunities unrelated to the organization's mission. When this occurs, it diverts valuable resources of the organization away from its mission. Any substantial diversion from an organization's purpose for existence will weaken employee loyalty and donor commitment. As a result, the organization can lose its sense of mission and accountability. But it is management's job to make sure this does not happen. Managers should pursue and welcome opportunities for acceleration or expansion of the organization's mission. Management, however, should reject anything that diverts the organization from fulfilling its mission.

Contractual accountability

Q Media Ministry agreed in writing to buy six months of air time from a television station for $10,000. However, after using the air time it refuses to pay the full amount because donations fell short of projections. Has Media Ministry breached its contract?

A Yes. Media Ministry has broken its promise to pay. If sued for collection, the ministry will have to pay the full $10,000. Unless Media Ministry's promise was expressly contingent on donation receipts, it did not act with integrity.

Another important measure of management's integrity is its commitment to keeping its promises. If anything should characterize a religious organization and its management, it should be *keeping promises*. This may be the toughest job to do. No matter. It is *essential* for any organization to keep its promises if it expects recognition as a credible organization. From an organizational perspective, contracts represent promises voluntarily entered into. And contract obligations are an important part of engaging in business and commercial transactions. Purchasing agents and other managers need not be attorneys, but they should understand basic contract accountability.

A *contract*, sometimes called an *agreement*, is made when two or more persons (or organizations) exchange promises. Each person relies on the other's promise as a basis for his or her own performance. The basic principles of a contract are easy to understand even by nonlawyers. The essence of a contract is the exchange of unambiguous promises to deliver what was promised at the time and place promised. Oral promises are as enforceable as written promises when they can be proved. But most people still prefer written contracts because oral promises are easy to forget and hard to prove.

The simplest way to remember the elements of a contract is to remember four Ps as follows:

☐ Parties: The parties to a contract are the people and organizations who make promises as part of the agreement. The contract should include the complete name and address of each party.

☐ Preambles: The preambles state the reasons why the parties are entering into the agreement.

☐ Promises: The promises specify what the parties promise to do, how and when they will do it, and what conditions will delay, hasten, or excuse their performance.

☐ Protections: These provisions are as important as any other part of the contract. They protect the integrity of the contract against the death of a party or the transfer of a party's interest. They specify which law governs when the contract needs to be interpreted. They state when the contract will end and how disputes may be resolved. They cover what happens if any party fails to keep a promise and define when the contract has been

breached. Protection clauses can also clarify what damages a
party may receive when another party is in breach.

▲

The important point to remember is that contracts contain
promises the parties intend to keep. What a party promises to
perform it should do, and what it promises to pay it should pay.
There is no excuse for failing to keep a promise, especially by any
religious organization claiming to promote fixed values. Keeping
one's word is the most basic of fixed values. Keeping promises is
a matter of personal and ministry integrity. Management publicly
shows its commitment to managing with integrity to the extent it
keeps its promises. The one who dwells with God, according to
Psalm 15, is the one "who keeps his oath even when it hurts."

There is no worse testimony for a ministry than to be known as
an organization that does not pay its bills when due. A ministry
may incur debts and make other promises in faith, believing that
God will provide the resources. When resources do not come in
as expected, the debts must still be paid in a timely fashion.
Creditors are not responsible to wait for God's provision to the
ministry. As God is faithful to keep his promises, so we must be
faithful to keep our promises.

It is rare for any organization to be truly unable to pay its debts
except when it is in a start-up phase. For an ongoing organization,
the problem is usually one of priorities rather than resources. For
most religious organizations, ministry is the number one priority.
This is a proper perspective, so long as debts incurred to fulfill the
organization's mission are viewed as part of its ministry as well.
Resources allocated to debt repayment should not be considered
nonministerial. The temptation to commit resources to ministerial
opportunities first and debts second must be resisted. It is up to
management to make sure debts are paid even if it means a cutback

in ministry activities. This is an attribute of organizational integrity.

Donor accountability

Q Evangelistic Association is a group of travelling evangelists affiliated with First Denomination. First Denomination requires each evangelist to pay ten percent of his or her annual income as a condition of good standing in the denomination. Evangelistic Association recently asked First Denomination how much the head minister of the denomination was paid. The denomination replied that the salary of the head minister is a secret. Has First Denomination shown its integrity and accountability?

A No. The salary of the head minister may be reasonable, but this is not the issue. The issue is whether First Denomination should demand financial integrity from its evangelists when it is unwilling to show its own integrity to them. Additionally, it is a question of whether First Denomination is willing to be transparent in its finances to avoid the appearance of impropriety.

Another measure of management's integrity is its commitment to keep its donors informed of the true financial condition of the organization. Donors are entitled to know how the organization will use their contributions by the organization. If donors ask how much the chief officer or any other manager is paid, tell them. It is a matter of integrity and of accountability. It is not because donors have a legal right to know, but because the organization recognizes that it owes donors integrity and accountability. This subject is discussed in greater detail in Chapter 14, Why Should Financial Disclosures Be Made?

8

Making Responsible Management Decisions

THERE ARE AT LEAST THREE REASONS WHY RELIGIOUS ORGANIZA-
tions are difficult to manage. First, they depend on uncertain
contributions to meet their budgetary needs. Second, they employ
many volunteers having varying degrees of commitment. Third,
they have no financial bottom line because they are not managed
to produce profits. Thus, it is difficult to measure religious organizations by traditional financial statement analysis. But
managers can still make responsible management decisions by
keeping the following guidelines in mind.

▮ Get information and counsel

Some people seem to manage with a bull whip and a chair, but
enlightened managers know that effective decision making
depends on an understanding of facts and available options. There
are some questions executive officers and other managers should
ask before making any management decision. Among these are:

- Do I have all the information I need?

- Is my information reliable and comprehensive?

- Will my decision advance the organization's mission?

There are few times when managers will have answers to all of their questions or even all the information needed to make a decision. But new situations seldom catch effective managers by surprise. They somehow manage to make an effective decision more often than an ineffective decision. They seem able to expect problems and opportunities before they arrive. How do they do it? The Bible has the answer: "Plans fail for lack of counsel, but with many advisers they succeed" (Proverbs 15:22).

Effective managers know how to prepare themselves to make decisions, solve problems, and grasp opportunities before the need arises. They do this by getting a steady stream of information from reliable sources. They constantly review and check this information before deciding. They prepare themselves with reliable information and decide on the basis of such information. They also do one other thing to get the right information: they seek professional counsel whenever the situation demands it.

How should management get professional advice and counsel when it confronts an important decision? First, look for a *competent* professional. Professional competence is usually measured by a person's education, experience, and reputation. For example, few people realize that most attorneys concentrate in certain areas of law, just as doctors specialize in certain areas of medicine. When an organization faces a bankruptcy matter, management should make sure it hires a lawyer who specializes in bankruptcy practice. A personal injury lawyer will not be competent in that area of practice.

If the organization receives a tax audit notice, it should consult a tax attorney or certified public accountant specializing in exempt organizations. An organization should always get the professional best suited to represent the interests of the organization and heed the advice given. The primary qualifications of a professional do not include whether he or she is a friend or relative of somebody in the organization. Nor do they include whether the professional will give a fee discount to the organization. The religion of the professional is a relevant factor, but not to the point of overriding competency issues. No one is entitled to a presumption of competency or integrity merely because he or she is a member of certain religious organizations.

▼

Finding, Hiring, and Working with a Professional

☐ Avoid hiring a relative or friend of the ministry.

☐ Ask other ministries, business people, chambers of commerce, or Christian professional associations to refer competent professionals specializing in the area of need.

☐ Interview prospective professionals and at a minimum ask for:

- A resume showing education and experience

- A list of representative clients

- Billing rates and methods of fee calculation

- A disclosure of any conflicts of interest

- A written retainer agreement including resolution of disputes by mediation or arbitration.

☐ Make a full disclosure of everything related to the matter requiring professional representation.

☐ Meet with the professional regularly to review progress and prepare to face the facts, information, and opinion he or she provides.

☐ Follow the professional's advice and pay his or her bills promptly after review and discussion.

▲

▌ Make ethical decisions

When managers get the information and professional opinions needed to make a decision, they should also ask whether certain options violate any law or ministry policy. Is each decision option consistent with personal standards of integrity? Will biblical values support each decision option? People, however, do not always realize when ethical issues are present. We all need to be more aware of ethical matters that come before us.

For example, a friend tells of when he was offered a lucrative business opportunity by a nonprofit organization that lobbied for pro-abortion political candidates. Since this friend opposes abortion, he wondered whether accepting the business was consistent with his personal values and would maintain his integrity. Upon reflection, he decided to reject the business opportunity. He did not want to service an organization whose mission was to support a position he opposes for moral and biblical reasons.

Before declining the business though, he asked his pastor and several friends for their opinion on the matter. All of them advised him to take the business. Several wondered why he would even think his integrity was at issue. This surprised him, not because their counsel was wrong or opposed to his own personal values, but because not one of his friends discussed the ethical issue at stake in this decision. All of his friends regularly attended church services and were committed to Christian principles. Still, not one of them gave advice in the light of biblical values!

Some say that managing an organization means getting things done through people, no matter what. But in a religious organization, such an approach sets the stage for ethical dilemmas. The test of good management is how well a person is able to fulfill the organization's goals efficiently and with integrity. When efficiency is elevated in priority over integrity, it presents an ethical problem.

Proper ethical decisions are the result of management's conscious adherence to fixed moral values. There is little evidence, however, to suggest that religious organizations make their management decisions any differently from other organizations. As George Gallup reported in 1987, "Church attendance makes little difference in people's ethical views and behavior; religious people lie, cheat, and pilfer as much as the nonreligious."

This is not to suggest that religious organizations make unethical management decisions. Rather, it is to affirm that religious organizations should set a higher standard and make ethical decisions on the basis of moral values that do not change with circumstances. Setting a higher standard, while difficult, should be the goal of all religious organizations. And it is not an unreasonable one since religious organizations provide moral guidance for individual decision making as part of their normal operations.

Evidence suggests that Jim Bakker and Richard Dortch, the now imprisoned former officers of PTL, lacked an understanding of fixed moral values. If they each had had a good sense of right and wrong on which to base personal and management decisions, neither would be in prison now. Yet it is not clear why they did not integrate fixed moral values into the fabric of their lives after years of service as Christian leaders.

A recent study by the Center for Business Ethics at Bentley College found that 91% of the major business corporations surveyed have written codes of ethics. Thirty-two percent of the companies surveyed have ethics committees as part of the

management team *(The Los Angeles Times,* June 3, 1990, p. D6).
Our survey of religious organizations did not try to determine how
many had written codes of ethics, but we did ask questions about
ethical issues. To our surprise we found that only one surveyed
organization had a written statement of core values (apart from
doctrinal statements of faith).

One organization focused on ethical concerns is the Executive
Leadership Foundation in Atlanta, Georgia. This organization is
pioneering ways to raise corporate America's awareness of the
need to make management decisions on the basis of fixed values.
The thrust of the foundation is to get business people "on course
with value systems and ethics derived from absolute values that
accept the divine connection." The view of the Executive Leadership Foundation is:

> the solution to our ethical dilemma today lies in voluntarily
> operating under the Authority which offers us an accountability,
> whose source transcends ourselves, and which is just, right and
> never-changing — a fixed and absolute base. God is that Source
> who can be trusted because His character never changes; it
> remains without variation or fluctuation today, yesterday, and
> forever. He is the ultimate Judge in discerning right from wrong.
> He is always just. What greater source for a value system could
> we possibly have than that which God divinely revealed? What
> greater base for a code of ethics than the law of God as
> summarized in the Ten Commandments? And, what better
> value base for leaders and followers could be found for the
> ethical conducting of business?

▮ **Be willing to admit mistakes**
Regardless of how thorough a manager is in getting information
or professional counsel and in examining ethical issues, some
decisions will still be poor decisions. They can be poor decisions
for many reasons: faulty information, a lack of facts, unforeseen

circumstances, and errors in judgment. Mistakes happen, and everyone makes them, including chief officers who make hundreds or thousands of management decisions every year. A good decision maker need only be right more often than wrong; no one will make the right decision every time.

The story of Classic Coke is a good example. The management of Coca Cola decided, after much research and market testing, to drop the original formula for Coke. It turned out to be a very poor decision and a marketing mistake. The management of Coca Cola quickly corrected the error in the face of consumer demand.

How could management make such a tremendous mistake? Obviously, the research and market testing was defective, but Coca Cola knew this only after the fact. The point, though, is what Coca Cola did when it became obvious it had made a wrong decision. Management admitted its error and turned the mistake into a market advantage by producing and distributing both Classic Coke and New Coke.

Ministry managers should respond similarly when facing the reality of having made a poor decision. When managers get all the available information and professional counsel needed and make the best decision possible, they have done all they can. Management duty has been fulfilled and the only thing left is to leave the results to God. If the decision turns out poorly, managers should admit it and turn it into an advantage. Then they should go on making the best management decisions possible.

Refer again to the General Standards of Conduct for Officers in Appendix B. Those standards state that an officer is entitled to rely on information and advice received from employees and outside professionals. Reliance on religious authorities by officers of religious organizations is expressly included. Thus, an officer is excused from liability to the organization and to any person when relying on this information or advice. A manager does not have to be perfect to act with integrity.

More commonly, though, ministry staff are likely to view the organization itself as immune to criticism. True, they acknowledge the organization has its imperfections, but these are always minimized. It is the unconverted and undiscipled people who always seem to have greater problems and command the ministry's attention. The organization's own shortcomings are never dealt with honestly. Ministry organizations rarely view their management problems as a priority. Outsiders who point out the ministry's problems are viewed as partners of the devil. Insiders who do the same are viewed as divisive. In the end, the ministry is glorified by people who are often motivated by insecurity. The ultimate result is idolatry.

Jesus' illustration of the good shepherd in Matthew 18 is an allegory for ministry management. The shepherd left the 99 sheep that were safe to find the one sheep that was lost. The shepherd/manager did not focus on the overwhelming presence of good sheep in his flock and pretend the lost sheep did not exist. It would not serve the best interests of the flock to boast how well the 99 sheep were doing and ignore the plight of the lost sheep. Finding the lost sheep was a matter of flock integrity.

It is the same for ministry management. Judgment begins with the household of God. We are to remove the log from our own eyes before trying to remove the speck in someone else's eye. If your religious organization has a management or integrity problem, clean it up rather than ignoring it! Honesty is still the best policy.

9

Ten Commandments for Ministry Management

Is YOUR RELIGIOUS ORGANIZATION MANAGED WITH INTEGRITY? THE original Ten Commandments contain many of the foundational principles of personal integrity and also can be applied to religious ministries in an organizational sense. When followed, these principles will enhance not only organizational accountability, but also ministry management.

■ **#1 Religious organizations are not independent.**

> "You shall have no other gods before me."
> *Exodus 20:3*

The key to individual morality is to realize that God is our Creator. He makes the rules that we must obey. No one is a law unto himself. That is why the first commandment says, "Have no other gods before me." Thus, personal accountability is related to how a person recognizes the sanctity of God's law. The same is true for organizations. Any organization that views itself as independent from the laws that bind the rest of society cannot commit itself to public accountability.

This is not to say that religious organizations are always accountable to government or the public for their actions. The issue of accountability is not one of immunity, but of equality. Regardless of who may have the right to enforce them, the rules of accountability are the same for everyone. Many laws apply to religious organizations on an equal basis with everyone else. Conduct that is unethical in business is also unethical in ministry. God is no respecter of persons or of organizations, and neither are the principles of integrity.

■ **#2 There are no exceptions to management accountability.**

> "You shall not make for yourself an idol."
> *Exodus 20:4*

The second commandment warns us not to make any idols for ourselves. Idolatry is not something religious organizations are immune to. Sometimes it is manifested in the adoration of the ministry head, who may be a commanding or charismatic personality. It's not that employees or donors are likely to actually worship the ministry head, because they would all recognize this as wrong. Yet, people sometimes view a ministry head as someone whose weaknesses are to be kept secret or ignored for the sake of the organization.

Just because a person has a vision for ministry does not mean he or she has the skills necessary to manage that ministry. While it may seem harsh, the reality is that having a confirmed vision for ministry does not entitle anyone to a presumption of perfect managerial judgment. It's interesting how often everyone knows the ministry head has managerial weaknesses, yet is treated as though none exist. In effect, the ministry head becomes idolized through the failure of donors and employees to challenge his or her judgment when it should be. Exceptions to the normal process of accountability always lead to trouble.

■ **#3 Management decisions are not divinely inspired.**

"You shall not misuse the name of the Lord your God."
Exodus 20:7

The third commandment directive not to misuse God's name is usually linked with the utterance of profanity, cursing, and swearing. Confirming this commandment, Jesus himself cautioned against the use of oaths. An oath is a form of swearing where God's name is used to add a sense of authority to what the speaker says. Jesus said to let your word stand on its own, a principle that upholds the sanctity of speech. This principle is also applicable to management decisions. In religious organizations these decisions are sometimes issued with the preface, "Thus says the Lord," or "God has told me . . ."

However, managers always have discretion when making decisions. Each management decision involves choosing the best means for accomplishing some ministry purpose. Although God defines the ultimate purposes for ministry, he leaves the choice of means up to us. He does not dictate which means to use and, therefore, he does not dictate management decisions. Adding God's name to a management decision is usually just a cloak to avoid accountability. After all, who dares to question the command of God? Using God's name to reduce management accountability is in opposition to organizational integrity.

■ **#4 Ministry personnel need to rest, too.**

"Remember the Sabbath day by keeping it holy."
Exodus 20:8

The Sabbath principle of the fourth commandment is based on the sanctity of rest. For the individual, this typically means that one day each week is set aside for a rest from vocational labor. The Sabbath is also a day for pursuing the worship of God rather than personal interests. Religious organizations need to keep this principle in mind for their staffs. Just because ministers and others in full-time religious service pursue religious activities daily does not make the Sabbath unnecessary.

This principle also recognizes that it is good to get away from the ministry once in a while. There is more to life than ministry, even for ministry staff. One benefit of resting is that it allows staff members to take a fresh look at what they are doing. This is true not only for ministry direction, but also for accountability. Resting from the daily flurry of activity is often the best way to rethink areas of ethical concern that were sidetracked at an earlier time.

▌ **#5 The family comes first, ministry comes second.**

"Honor your father and your mother."
Exodus 20:12

The fifth commandment to honor parents is a moral command for the young and old alike. The child honors his parents, who provide for his every need, by his obedience. The adult honors his parents by providing for them when they can no longer provide for themselves. The commandment implicitly recognizes that the family is the basic building block of society—not the government, the church, or religious ministry. Nurturing and protecting the ability of staff personnel to care for their family members is a priority of every ministry.

However, religious organizations often expect their staff to work for less income than what they would earn performing the same job for someone else. Yet, these same staff people may serve the ministry by helping operate ministry business activities supported by sales rather than donations. This creates a role reversal, where the family's provision for its members takes second place to the ministry's running of its own business. It would make more sense to help ministry staff be better at providing for their own families. When this is done, staff members will give the ministry better service and ultimately increase the integrity of the organization.

▌ #6 There is more to life than ministry.

"You shall not murder."
Exodus 20:13

For the individual, committing murder is not only a moral wrong, but a most serious crime warranting the strictest punishment. Accordingly, the purpose of the sixth commandment is to protect the sanctity of life. This same principle applies to religious organizations in the sense that life apart from ministry has a high value and is not to be demeaned. Thus, there is no reason to view someone who leaves the staff or membership of a religious organization as good as dead.

This is especially true for people who leave an organization because they have met problems no one seems willing to resolve or even acknowledge. From an accountability standpoint, the branding of all former staff as heretics usually betrays a serious problem in management integrity. The same is occasionally true when there is a high ministry staff turnover rate. The solution is for management to face up to the problem, not to snub anyone who knows about it and might tell others. Any organization that operates with integrity has nothing to fear from staff who leave, and no reason to feel ill toward them.

■ **#7 Religion and business make awkward partners.**

"You shall not commit adultery."
Exodus 20:14

The seventh commandment, like the fifth commandment, is directed at maintaining the integrity of the family unit. The prohibition of adultery upholds the sanctity of marriage and faithfulness to one's first love. In addition, adultery is used as a metaphor in the Bible to describe not only individual infidelity, but also corporate unfaithfulness. Both ancient Israel and the prophetic church are denounced for their infidelity. This same concept can be applied to religious organizations today.

However, the present focus is not on the pursuit of false religion, but on the pursuit of nonreligion, namely, unrelated business activities. When a ministry engages in unrelated business activities, it has begun the process of leaving its first love. Of necessity, a portion of the ministry's staff, money, and time are diverted to the pursuit of activities unrelated to its nonprofit/religious/tax-exempt mission. When a ministry does not stay true to its primary mission, it eventually reduces the level of organizational accountability. Unrelated business activity is not simply a question of tax liability, but of management integrity.

■ **#8 Don't give to God what belongs to someone else.**

"You shall not steal."
Exodus 20:15

The eighth commandment's prohibition of stealing is one of the more easily overlooked commandments. One common form of theft is the making of unauthorized copies of copyrighted material. Religious and other organizations sometimes promote the view that they are excused from copyright laws if the copied material is used for a nonprofit purpose. A rarer form of abuse occurs when an organization persuades its members to transfer all of their personal property to the ministry. In each case, however, the organization has shown a lack of respect for the sanctity of private property.

Other forms of theft are more subtle. Jesus condemned the practice of Corban, in which people merely declared some of their property to be set apart for ministry. The problem was that the original owners kept the full control and possession of these so-called ministerial assets. Corban was a form of theft in that people kept for themselves what belonged to God. This is a danger when the ministry receives donated property, such as jewelry, that the ministry head decides to keep for personal use instead of selling. When an organization maintains nonministerial assets for the personal use of its leaders, such as resort condominiums and limousines, the result is much the same.

❚ #9 Don't promise what you cannot deliver.

> "You shall not give false testimony."
> *Exodus 20:16*

One of the hallmarks of individual integrity is keeping every promise that has been made, even when it later proves to be disadvantageous. Thus, the ninth commandment prohibits any false testimony, whether it concerns something the speaker has seen or something the speaker will do. A person is held accountable for giving a false witness *(perjury)* or breaking a promise *(breach of contract)*. Organizations are no less accountable for the testimony they give to staff, members, vendors, and donors.

It is a sad commentary on the state of religious ministry when "evangelistically speaking" is a metaphor for wholesale exaggeration. Repeated or flagrant exaggeration is nothing other than the testimony of a false witness. Telling the truth (making full disclosure) allows for no compromise when describing ministry activities, individual responses shown, money raised, or how funds are being used. And, there is no greater barrier to an effective religious witness than a ministry's reputation for paying creditors late. For the sake of management integrity, don't promise what you cannot deliver.

▌ **#10 Don't worry about keeping up with the competition.**

> "You shall not covet."
> *Exodus 20:17*

For individuals, the tenth commandment against coveting is a key to maintaining purity of mind, another aspect of personal integrity. The commandment implicitly recognizes that lustful thoughts lead to wrong choices and actions. Ministries can suffer from a similar form of lustful thinking when they want what other organizations have. It is easy to envy ministries that have recently upgraded facilities, the ability to raise funds, or a certain prestige in the religious community. Coveting the fringe benefits of ministry's success can be a snare to any religious organization.

What coveting often leads to is the recommendation of ministry action by management without properly checking things out first. For example, another ministry may have several profitable business activities. However, do not assume the other ministry has received the proper tax advice and all necessary government approvals. The other ministry may collapse after a tax audit in a few months. Management should never let coveting lead to a failure to be diligent. The managers of each organization have a responsibility to check things out for themselves. Integrity and accountability are best served by letting proper information and counsel, rather than a mere desire to keep pace, drive ministry activities.

10
When Ministries Go into Business

MANY PEOPLE IN ORGANIZED MINISTRY BELIEVE THAT THE REGULA-
tion of religious organizations by government is increasing all the
time, and they are probably right. However, ministries should not
view all government regulation as a form of persecution, even if
it seems like a form of suffering. Not all suffering is the result of
persecution, and not all regulation is an unwarranted invasion of
the religious sphere. It is not necessary to characterize all un-
pleasantness as an attack by satanic forces.

Regulation, like suffering, is of two kinds. First Peter 4:15-17
informs us, "If you suffer, it should not be as a murderer or thief
or any other kind of criminal, or even as a meddler. However, if
you suffer as a Christian, do not be ashamed, but praise God that
you bear that name." Thus, there are two kinds of suffering people
can face. First, people can suffer when they have given others
cause to intervene in their affairs. Second, people can suffer when

others persecute them without cause. One must know the difference between these two.

Undoubtedly, some regulation is the result of anti-Christian and anti-religious sentiments promoted by certain public officials. This oppressive regulation and other forms of official persecution are the subjects of Chapter 16. Business regulation, though, is not a form of persecution. It is merely the natural result of conducting business. This does not mean that business activities carried on by ministries are evil (that is, they are not like criminal activities). Business activities nevertheless give public officials cause to examine ministry affairs.

All about Business and Ministry

Religious organizations today engage in a wide variety of economic enterprise. They conduct many kinds of activities and raise funds from many kinds of sources. Most ministries no longer support themselves exclusively by donations. Much of modern religious ministry occurs through items that are sold, such as books, tapes, videos, T-shirts, and computer programs. Donations still play an important part in religious ministry, especially among churches. But donation revenues no longer dominate the religious field as they once did.

Furthermore, business activities are not the exclusive domain of parachurch ministries. A local church is as likely to own or control business activities with a religious focus as is a parachurch group. These include day-care centers, private schools and colleges, retirement villages, and religious conference and retreat centers. Add to this the proliferation of religious services for sale, such as counseling, teaching seminars, and media services. Some ministries are simply organizations that sell exclusively religious products and services to exclusively religious clients. It is not merely parachurch groups that have gone free enterprise, but the whole of religion.

The purpose of the present discussion is to show that business regulation is a natural part of conducting business. Another purpose is to help explain why this is the case. It is no mere coincidence that as religious business activity has increased, government regulation of religion has also increased. What is it that distinguishes business activities from religious ministry? And, what is it about business activities that makes them subject to government regulation?

Religious ministry is a form of charity

Giving time, energy, and wealth to others is part of our nature. Certainly, it is God's nature to give these things to us. Since all people are made in God's image, it is our nature to follow his example in giving to others. Yet, even though God wants us to give, he does not force anyone to give. Every gift is voluntary, not obligatory. Every gift is ruled by love, not legal duty.

The essence of love is to be unselfish and to prefer the welfare of others. According to Luke 6:35, "love your enemies, do good to them, and lend to them without expecting to get anything back." True charity is always a work of giving motivated by love. In fact, charity is merely another word for love. All religious ministry that is a work of giving motivated by love is also charitable. The hallmark of traditional ministry is providing religious services to the public freely, as a gift. This is why federal tax law normally classifies religious organizations as charities (or, nonprivate foundations) today.

An aspect of all charity is that it fulfills a moral duty that only God can enforce. Religious ministry cannot be compelled by anyone, whether by a public official or by any private person. After all, if God does not force us either to love or to give, how could anyone else do so? Therefore, any payment made under a contract is not based on love, but on obligation. Similarly, so-called contributions that are made to satisfy a debt are not really gifts at all. This sets the stage for an important distinction between things that are ministry activities and things that are business activities.

Business activity is the opposite of charity

Since a gift is always motivated by love rather than obligation, it can never involve a required exchange. A purchase or sale, on the other hand, always involves an exchange. People sell things only to receive something back. Sales transactions are not acts of love, charity, or ministry. There is not only a big difference between a gift and a sale, but they are opposites. The same can be said about ministry and business.

In Deuteronomy 23 the Israelites were told not to charge interest on loans made to their countrymen, though they could charge interest to foreigners. A similar distinction was made about debt cancellation in Deuteronomy 15. Why was this distinction made between Israelites and foreigners? Fellow Israelites were regarded as brothers whose relationships were governed by love, so charity prevailed. Transactions with foreigners were not ruled by love, so business customs prevailed. The distinction was not so much between Israelites and nonIsraelites, as it was between charity (ministry) and business. This distinction still has importance today.

It is important to recognize things for what they truly are, not merely the way we might want them to be. Not all activities of religious organizations are necessarily ministry activities. An activity is not religious just because someone calls it ministry, when it is really business. Any time a fee must be paid as a condition of receiving products or services, the transaction is a sale rather than a gift. Whenever sales are made, the character of the activity is business, not ministry. School tuition, day-care fees, religious auditing fees, admission charges to resorts, and rental fees for retirement villages are all business transactions.

Q Evangelistic Association recently put on a country fair to raise funds for its ministry. General admission to the fair was $5 and amusement rides were an additional $1 each. People without tickets were not admitted. The fair was a huge success, and raised $50,000 for the ministry after expenses. Was the fair a religious ministry or a business activity of Evangelistic Association?

A It was a business activity. The money raised did not come from donations, but from ticket sales. Providing amusement rides is not a ministry activity. A big clue to whether an activity is ministry or business is to determine whether the revenues it generates are deductible as contributions. If revenues are not deductible as contributions, the activity is part of a business.

This does not mean that ministry and business are incompatible in any way. The point here is not to demean religious business activities, nor is it to push religious organizations into a former way of operating. Rather it is simply to point out that religious ministry and business activities are inherently different in character. A religious organization may conduct both religious ministry and business activities if it wants to. But when an organization enters the field of business, however motivated, it should expect to be treated like a business and not like a ministry.

Business activities bring government regulation

The reason for identifying an activity as business rather than ministry is solely to help explain why one can expect government regulation of that activity. This is true even when the business activity is related to the organization's exempt purposes. Regulation does not mean that the activity is wrong, unrelated, or taxable. It only means that it is business, not religious ministry. Government regulation is a natural part of all business activity.

Certainly, religious organizations have enjoyed some exemptions created for them in the business arena in the past. One significant exemption is the nontaxation of income from related business activities. Nonexempt organizations, of course, are taxed on all business activities. Thus, religious organizations have a special exemption that is to their advantage. There is a problem, though, when knowledge of this exemption creates an expectation (often unrealistic) that spills over into other areas.

For example, ministries sometimes assume that federal tax exemption also exempts the organization from state sales taxes or property taxes. But in many states this is not true. Nor are religious organizations exempt from many other forms of business regulation. Many schools and day-care centers operated by religious organizations are regulated the same as those operated by profit corporations. Laws about assumed business names and business licensing usually apply to religious organizations as well. There is simply no general exemption for religious organizations from laws applicable to all others. In fact, the trend may be to cut back on the exemptions that now exist.

When organizations engage in business activities of any kind, they can expect governmental regulation to follow, regardless of the nature of the business. The only way to avoid business regulation is to avoid business activities. Enduring government regulation is simply one of the costs of doing business. If you cannot stand the heat of government business regulation, then get out of business. Do not view business regulation as a form of religious persecution.

For the most part, business regulation is no respecter of persons. One does not avoid business regulation because one is a Christian. Nor do organizations avoid regulation because they are religious. When an organization enters the field of business, it generally does so on an equal footing with all other businesses. When exemptions are granted, this is a matter of privilege, not a right.

Business Regulation Brings More Accountability

Since business activities bring more government regulation, they necessarily also bring more governmental accountability. That is, organizations are accountable to government to the extent they engage in business activities. As every business person knows, our public officials have not been lax in finding new ways to further regulate businesses. Three of these regulations commonly apply to business activities of religious organizations:

Sales taxes and licenses

Most states have some sort of *sales tax* and *use tax*. A sales tax applies whenever there is a retail sale in the state. A retail sale is a sale of some product or service to the final consumer. A use tax applies to the consumption of items in the state that are bought out of state. The two taxes normally apply to the same kinds of goods and services and are at the same rates within the same state. A single transaction is subject to only one tax or the other, not both.

Sellers of products and services usually must register with any state in which they are located. They must also get a license to make sales and collect the sales and use taxes. Since sales and use taxes apply only to sales and purchases, they apply only to business activities. No sales tax license needs to be secured by religious organizations that make no sales. Thus, sales and use taxes do not pertain to ministry activities. When a religious organization must collect sales or use taxes, it is acting in the capacity of a business.

Most states have exemptions from sales and use taxes for certain kinds of transactions. Various states exempt purchases made by religious organizations, sales made by them, or both. Some states exempt sales of certain items, such as newspapers or Bibles, regardless of who sells them. Exemptions are different in every state, as are tax rates and licensing requirements. Recently, both sales tax exemptions for religious literature and sales taxes imposed on religious organizations have been the subject of U.S. Supreme Court cases.

In *Swaggart Ministries v. California,* a 1989 case, state authorities imposed sales and use taxes on the sale of religious books, tapes, and other materials. Swaggart Ministries opposed the tax solely on the basis that taxing religious materials violated its religious freedom. The Supreme Court, however, upheld the taxes. It ruled that the Constitution does not shelter religious organizations from taxes generally applicable to everyone else.

Some people in ministry have feared that this case has broken down a part of the wall separating church and state. This fear is unwarranted. Just because the seller was a religious organization selling religious materials to church members does not convert the sales activity into ministry. Since paying a certain price was a condition to receiving the desired materials, the activity was in the nature of business. No organization can complain when the government merely recognizes business activity for what it truly is and treats it the same as business activity carried on by others.

Another recent case, *Texas Monthly v. Bullock* (1989), considered whether a sales tax exemption for religious periodicals in Texas was constitutional. The Supreme Court held that the exemption was invalid because its sole purpose was to help organized religion. This holding is not a form of religious persecution. It merely recognizes that sales by religious organizations can be taxed the same as sales by anyone else. It does, however, foreshadow the chance that future similar exemptions may be invalidated. This possibility should not be dismissed lightly.

Taken together, the *Swaggart* and *Texas Monthly* cases affirm that religious organizations will tend to be treated the same as anyone else when operating in the business arena. Put another way, the Supreme Court does not view the sale of products or services as religious ministry. States may exempt religious organizations if they want to (in limited situations), but they can also take these exemptions away. In the end, if religious organizations want to engage in business, they can expect to be regulated the same as other business organizations.

State and federal securities laws

A ministry may occasionally desire to sell investment units to finance a large project. For example, a church may sell bonds to finance a building program. An organization may sell interests in retirement village apartments, or even time-share units in a resort condominium community. Though these transactions may help some broadly defined religious goals, they are really business transactions in nature. Therefore, expect that they may be covered by some form of business regulation.

A form of business regulation often overlooked by religious organizations is securities regulation. A *security* includes any form of investment unit in an organization, such as shares of stock in a corporation. Each state has a securities law (often called a *Blue Sky Law)* that regulates sales made either to buyers or by sellers located in that state. In addition, most all securities sales are regulated by federal securities laws. There are actually two federal securities laws—one that regulates sales similar to state laws, and the other that regulates stock exchanges.

Securities laws regulate all sales of investments except those that are specifically exempted. Non-exempt investments must be subject to prior review and approval by public officials, or accompanied by a lengthy and technical disclosure document, or both. Even exempt securities sales are often exempt only from the review and approval process, not from the disclosure requirements. Investments sold without following securities laws may result in both monetary fines and jail sentences for the unwary. Before selling any kind of investment unit, an organization should consult with a securities law expert.

The federal securities act, for example, does exempt all securities sold by any nonprofit religious or charitable organization. However, this exemption is lost if the organization engages in any non-exempt activities that are substantial in nature. It also does not apply if promoters can profit from the sale of the investment units. Just because a security is exempt at the federal level does not mean it is exempt at the state level. In California, securities sold by religious organizations are exempt from regulation except if they are money-lending agreements or *debt instruments*. Hence, the sale of church bonds would not be exempt from regulation in that state.

Securities regulation is usually more of a concern whenever a religious organization has one or more subsidiary corporations that are for profit. Even the shares of stock issued to the ministry when the subsidiary is formed are regulated by law. Permission may need to be obtained from a state agency before the subsidiary can issue its shares. Securities regulation is virtually unavoidable whenever investment units are sold that directly or indirectly benefit a profit subsidiary.

Q City Church wants to build and operate a resort condominium village as part of its expanding ministry program. City Church has an annual budget of $4,000,000, and wishes to raise about $10,000,000 for the project. The village will include a chapel that will have regular religious services and employ a full-time pastor on premises to minister to the residents. Investment counsel has advised City Church that selling limited partnership units would be the best way to finance the building project. In addition, maintenance costs could be financed by selling time-share interests in the condos. What should the board of City Church do?

A Hire the services of a competent securities lawyer. Both the limited partnership units and the time-share interests are securities. Since the project budget is substantial compared to City Church's normal operating budget, the securities may not be exempt even under federal law. This is a risk because operating a resort condominium village is likely to be viewed as a nonexempt activity. Lengthy disclosure documents and securities registration may be needed.

Unrelated business taxable income

A form of business regulation that is perhaps more familiar to many ministries is the *unrelated business income tax* (UBIT). Once it is determined that an activity is *business* rather than ministry, the next step is to determine whether it is related to the organization's exempt purposes. Business activities *related* to an organization's exempt purposes are not taxed. Revenues derived from business activities that are *unrelated* to any exempt purpose must be reported on a Form 990-T. This is true even if the organization is otherwise exempt from filing a regular Form 990, the annual information return for exempt organizations. Profits from unrelated businesses are taxed at normal corporate rates, even though the organization is otherwise tax exempt.

Federal tax law generally requires that any exempt organization be organized and operated *exclusively* for exempt purposes. Failure to meet this requirement is grounds for the IRS to refuse or revoke an organization's exempt status. But this rule is not quite as restrictive as it seems. Tax regulations have interpreted the rule as requiring only that an exempt organization must be engaged *primarily* in exempt activities. No more than an insubstantial amount of the organization's activities can further any purpose unrelated to an exempt purpose. A ministry needs to examine carefully what activities are *unrelated* and when such activities are no longer *insubstantial*.

According to tax regulations, a trade or business that is regularly carried on is unrelated to an exempt purpose when it "is not substantially related (other than through the production of funds) to the organization's performance of its exempt functions." To be related to an exempt purpose, an activity must "contribute importantly" to an exempt purpose.

An *unrelated* trade or business does not include activities:

• performed for the organization without pay

- carried on primarily for the convenience of members or employees

- consisting of the resale of donated merchandise.

Obviously, apart from these three instances, the test for relatedness is not a bright line or "litmus paper" kind of test. It depends on all the facts and circumstances surrounding an activity. One thing to be said, though, is that business income is not related to an exempt purpose merely because profits are used for ministry activities. The business activity that generates the profits must itself serve an exempt purpose, or the profits will be taxable.

Q Parachurch, Inc. (an exempt organization) has been given several apartment buildings by various donors. Instead of converting these units to a different use, the ministry has decided to collect the rents from tenants and otherwise act as a landlord. Is the income from this activity taxable to Parachurch, Inc.?

A Yes. Assuming the rental of apartments is regularly carried on, such activity is a trade or business that serves no religious purpose. Whether Parachurch, Inc. uses the profits to fund ministry activities is irrelevant. The revenues must be reported on a Form 990-T and the profits, if any, will be taxable.

The presence of unrelated business activities that are regularly carried on may not pose any problem to some religious organizations. Such ministries have the administrative capacity to handle the extra reporting requirements and the extra resources to pay any tax liability. For other organizations, though, these burdens may be heavy. This is especially true for churches and religious orders that are normally exempt from filing Form 990. However, every ministry must be on guard that its unrelated business activities do not become substantial compared to its overall activities. When this happens, the organization's tax-exempt status is in jeopardy.

Whether unrelated activities are substantial or not also depends on the facts and circumstances surrounding the activity. There are few concrete tests and no specific percentage levels to guide organizations in this inquiry. The two actual cases below will illustrate the uncertainty in this area, but may provide some general guidance as to when unrelated activities become substantial.

- Scripture Press Foundation published and sold religious books and pamphlets at competitive market prices. The organization claimed it qualified for exempt status, but the Court of Claims disagreed (1961). The court found that the sale of religious literature is a business activity unrelated to any exempt religious purpose. And since this activity accounted for all of the organization's revenues, it was substantial compared to the organization's total activities. Exempt status was denied.

- World Family Corporation was organized as a tax-exempt religious organization to provide financial aid to missionaries. As a subordinate activity, the ministry allocated 10% of its total expenses to fund certain scientific research. The Tax Court (1983) decided that the research activity was insubstantial in relation to the organization's tax-exempt religious activities. While this case provides some insight as to when an activity may be viewed as insubstantial, it should not be regarded as a safe harbor. The Tax Court was well aware that its decision might be interpreted this way. Thus, in a footnote, it said it was not trying to establish a general rule for future cases in finding 10% of total expenses to be insubstantial.

In summary, related business activities are not taxable nor do they jeopardize tax-exempt status. The rule regarding UBIT is that unrelated business activities regularly carried on are taxable at the normal corporate rate and must be reported on a Form 990-T. Substantial unrelated business activities that are regularly carried on jeopardize the exempt status of a religious organization. They must be stopped or divested to prevent a revocation of exemption.

The problem, of course, is that it is not always a simple matter to determine whether a business activity is related or unrelated. Nor is it always clear what is substantial or insubstantial from an IRS perspective. The most conservative course for a religious organization is to avoid all business activities whether related or not, and engage solely in religious ministry activities. However, with proper counsel, a ministry may nonetheless engage in some business activities without an undesirable tax impact.

One final caveat—the presence of any unrelated business activity may have an unintended impact in non-income tax areas. For example, participation in some charitable donation campaigns for government employees requires that an organization not have any unrelated business activities at all. Many states deny sales tax and property tax exemptions for activities of a religious organization that are unrelated to its exempt purposes. Some states even condition favored status under workers' compensation and unemployment compensation laws on the absence of any unrelated activities. Accordingly, avoiding all unrelated business activities may be better in the long term, even if it deprives an organization of a source of funds.

What Happens When Religion and Business Are Mixed?

Part of the benefit of drawing a clear distinction between religious ministry and business activities is that the accountability concerns of any organization are also clearly defined. When an organization performs solely religious ministry, it is immune to most forms of regulation. Organizational accountability for ministry runs solely to God and to those in authority in the organization. Any government intrusion into this sphere can be vigorously contested. On the other hand, any business activity inevitably carries with it a certain amount of government regulation. Accountability for business activities runs to government as well as to the organization itself. Further, the organization is accountable to "customers" who have a legal, not merely a moral, right to get what they pay for and to enforce their sales contracts.

This clear distinction is muddied, however, when ministries engage in a variety of activities intended to combine ministry and business in a single enterprise. Everyone, including organization members, purchasers, and public officials, expects to demand some accountability because of the business aspects of the activity. The ministry, however, may wish to disclaim all of these because it views the activity as part of its religious ministry. The organization can be torn in several directions at once, recognizing that the demands of government, members, and purchasers may conflict with each other. Yet this is a situation created by the ministry's own choice to mix ministry with business—how can it complain about the undesirable results?

The part-gift part-sale program
One of the more common forms of mixing ministry with business occurs in the part-gift part-sale program. This occurs whenever an organization solicits funds by offering to send the donor an item of merchandise that has a value less than the payment. In effect, the part of the payment equal to the value of the merchandise is a purchase, and the excess is a donation. The ministry is clearly soliciting a gift, but it is also clearly bound to send the item. The matter is even more clearly like a sale when the ministry refuses to send the item unless a minimum contribution is first received.

When the value of the item is insubstantial compared to the total payment, it is referred to as a premium. The value of the premium item is disregarded for tax purposes and the entire payment is treated as a deductible donation. The IRS has recently issued new guidelines for handling premiums (Revenue Procedure 90-12, attached as Appendix I). Under these guidelines, charities must inform donors how much of their payment is a deductible contribution. And the value of the premium cannot exceed 2% of the payment or $50, whichever is less. Alternatively, certain items (such as bookmarks, key chains, etc.) always have an insubstantial value if the payment is $25 or more. The guidelines also include several examples.

A related program is where merchandise having a substantial value is sold at inflated prices, with the surplus value intended to be treated as a contribution. A book may be sold for twice its value, or a dinner plate may be sold for four times its value. The concept is the same as using premium incentives, except that the value of the item is not insubstantial. Thus, the ministry must calculate and inform patrons how much of their payment is deductible, because not all of it will be.

As long as a religious organization keeps within IRS guidelines and informs donors of the deductible portion of their payments, this kind of program is fairly benign. There is always the risk that donors will complain about the quality of the item they receive for their payments, but this risk tends to be small on the average. Other forms of mixing ministry and business are not so benign, however.

Charitable investment schemes

Consider the following funds solicitation proposal. A religious organization wants to raise $500,000 to secure an office building. It solicits people who might be willing to lend money to the ministry in multiples of $5,000 for ten years. After ten years, the ministry must repay the lenders a principal amount that is the amount of the loan or the building's market value, whichever is less. Interest accrues in an amount equal to the lesser of 9%

compounded annually, or the excess of the market value of the building over the principal amount computed above.

If the value of the building appreciates, the lenders will be paid a maximum of their original loan plus 9% interest. If the building's value depreciates, the lenders get only the current value returned without interest. The question is whether this transaction is intended to be a donation or an investment. It could be argued either way, depending on whether the building appreciates (investment) or depreciates (donation). Actually, it is intended to be both.

This mixing of business and charitable elements in a single transaction confuses things considerably. Lenders will be unsure whether to report any interest income for the first nine years. They also will not be certain whether they are entitled to any contribution deductions by reason of the loan until the ten years has expired. Several years of amended tax returns may have to be filed. The ministry, meanwhile, has the potential for realizing some debt-financed (taxable) income when the property is sold, depending on various factors. The loans will probably be viewed as debt instruments requiring securities laws compliance.

Not all activities that mix business and ministry are this complex, of course, nor are they all as benign as offering premium incentives. In each case, however, the introduction of business elements will increase the amount of regulation any transaction is subject to. It may simply require telling donors of the amount of their contribution or getting a sales tax license. Or, it may require the preparation of bulky securities disclosure documents. In any event, such regulation should not be viewed as a form of religious persecution. Rather, it is merely the cost of doing business.

11

How to Avoid Ten IRS Land Mines

THE DRIVE TO INCREASE REVENUE LEADS MANY RELIGIOUS ORGANI-
zations to start up business activities. Easy profits are expected,
but tax traps waiting to spring could result in hefty taxes even for
a tax-exempt organization. Business activities of ministries bring
other problems along as well, such as new administrative burdens
and reporting requirements. Some nonbusiness activities can also
create the possibility of taxable income even though the organization is otherwise tax exempt. Still other activities can remove the
deductibility of certain contributions or even jeopardize the entire
ministry's tax-exempt status. Keep an eye on the tax laws, and
watch out for the following IRS land mines!

▌ **Avoid engaging in unrelated business activities.**
Sometimes religious organizations engage in business activities
that help them fulfill some ministry purpose. These business
activities are known as *related business activities* because they
advance an exempt purpose of the organization. It is permissible
for a religious organization to have related business activities from

an IRS perspective. The net income from such activities is not taxable.

Q City Church decides to sell tapes of its pastor's sermons to the congregation at cost plus a minimum mark-up. City Church believes selling these tapes helps minister to the congregation by declaring the principles of the Christian faith. The profit from sales is put into the general operating budget. Is the sale of these tapes related to the religious purposes of City Church?

A Yes. The profit from sales is not subject to federal income tax because the business activity is related to the exempt purposes of City Church. However, the gross sales revenues may still be subject to state sales taxes.

On the other hand, *unrelated business activities* are activities that do not help fulfill any tax-exempt purpose of an organization. Unrelated business activities are never necessary for religious ministry—that is what makes them unrelated. Therefore, an exempt organization needs to report unrelated activities to the IRS. Every religious organization having unrelated business activities must file an IRS Form 990-T for income received from unrelated business activity. This includes churches and religious orders (which are exempt from filing an IRS Form 990). The organization will also incur extra administrative and reporting expenses because of its activities. It will also need to make disclosure of things it would not otherwise need to tell the IRS.

Of course, the religious organization must pay any applicable tax on the unrelated business income. This also adds to the administrative burden, since costs must now be allocated between taxable and exempt activities. If unrelated activities become substantial compared to total activities, the religious organization may even lose its tax-exempt status. It is not unusual for sales tax and other state tax exemptions to be made expressly inapplicable to an organization's unrelated business activities.

Q Missions Board opens a religious bookstore in a local shopping center. The bookstore sells only religious books and materials including teaching tapes prepared by its head minister. All items are sold at normal retail prices. All profit from sales is put into the general operating budget of Missions Board. Is operating this bookstore related to the religious ministry of Missions Board?

A No. The IRS views retail religious bookstores as profit-seeking businesses much like any other bookstore. Profit-seeking businesses are unrelated to the exempt purposes of a religious organization. Not only are the gross sales subject to state sales tax, but the profits are subject to state and federal income taxes. Further, Missions Board must file a Form 990-T to report the income from its bookstore.

▌ Avoid the sale of advertising to outside companies.
Many ministries publish their own newsletters, magazines, and catalogs designed to minister to the spiritual needs of the reader. If these publications promote only the products and services of the publishing organization there is little to be concerned about. However, if the ministry accepts paid advertising from other organizations, the advertising fees may be unrelated business taxable income. Whether taxes will actually be payable depends on the extent of offsetting deductions available.

The reason this tax potential exists is that advertising is usually not related to any religious or other exempt purpose. It does not matter that the publication is a *religious* magazine, the publisher is a *religious* organization, the advertiser is a *religious* organization, and the product or service advertised is a *religious* item. Even when this is the case, the act of selling advertising is not itself a religious activity. Rather, it is a sale of a business service (advertising) that is taxed like a business is taxed. This is the general rule, to which there are some very limited exceptions. Consult your ministry's tax professional for specific tax advice.

▌ Avoid noncash donations that are debt-financed property.

Q Media Ministry accepts the donation of a twelve-unit apartment building subject to a 2-year-old debt of $500,000. Media Ministry agrees to take over the debt and promptly sells the property for $750,000. Must Media Ministry file an IRS Form 990-T and pay federal income tax on the gain?

A Yes. The debt on the building existed when the donation was made and is acquisition indebtedness. This means the building is debt-financed property. The gain of $250,000 (less applicable expenses) is unrelated debt-financed income, and is taxable.

A ministry need not engage in any actual business activities to be liable for federal income taxes. Noncash property that is *debt-financed property* may result in liability for income taxes when the property is sold. Generally speaking, debt-financed property is any noncash property acquired subject to *acquisition indebtedness*. Debt-financed property includes real estate subject to debt at the time of ministry acquisition, even if the ministry has not agreed to pay it. The income realized from the sale of debt-financed property is called *unrelated debt-financed income*. This is true even if the noncash property was acquired by the ministry as a donation.

The debt-financed property rule is one reason to avoid accepting some noncash donations subject to a debt. However, this tax can be avoided if the debt is over five years old when the ministry receives the property. The tax also does not apply if the property is put to an exempt use by the ministry within a certain time after acquisition. There are other limitations and variations to the debt-financed property rule that management should discuss with the ministry's tax advisor. An organization can flag potential tax problems by preparing, in advance, written guidelines for considering noncash donations.

█ **Avoid dealing with related organizations except at arms' length.**

Some religious organizations divide their operations among multiple corporations. There are a variety of reasons for doing this. A related organization may carry out unrelated business activities. Or, it may be useful for borrowing large amounts of money. Other organizations may engage in political activities. Some operations may be state-licensed or federally funded and are best kept separate from the main ministry. However, ministries often view all related organizations as being under a single ministry umbrella for fund-raising or administrative purposes. Separate organizations may all be housed in the same building. Legal distinctions often are ignored in the day-to-day management of the overall ministry.

This often results in dealings between organizations that are not at "arms' length." That is, they do not deal with each other the same way they would with outside vendors or other disinterested third parties. A ministry may lend money to a related organization at an interest rate below the normal market rate. This could result in additional taxable interest income being imputed to the ministry. This is especially likely where the related organization is a profit corporation controlled by an exempt ministry organization. Favorable loan terms extended by the ministry could also be private inurement if the borrowing organization has any outside stockholders. Watch out!

█ Avoid *assignment of income* problems.

Ministry staff, particularly ministry leaders, often write books. Or, they may make recordings or create other works of authorship in their own names that produce royalty income. Sometimes authors wish to assign all or part of the royalty rights, but not the underlying copyright, to their ministry organization. They usually intend to avoid having to pay income taxes on that money personally. However, unless the assignment is made correctly, the author will remain personally liable for income taxes on the royalties paid to the ministry. An effective assignment must be both permanent (irrevocable) and a transfer of the author's entire interest in the underlying work to the ministry.

> **Q** The national director of Evangelistic Association has written a best-selling book for which she holds the copyright. To avoid paying income taxes on the book royalties she assigns her royalty rights to Evangelistic Association, but retains the copyright. Does this assignment of royalty rights shift the tax liability for the royalties to Evangelistic Association?

> **A** No. The national director has not transferred her entire interest in the book to the ministry. However, if she irrevocably assigns the copyright, royalty rights, and all other interest she has in the book to Evangelistic Association, she will avoid personal liability for income taxes on the royalties.

A similar situation arises when a ministry assigns a portion of its income to a subsidiary corporation. Suppose a ministry forms a related organization solely to report unrelated business taxable income generated by the activities of ministry staff. Unless the related organization owns the assets and proprietary rights of the business, the assignment of income will not shift any tax liability.

To shift taxable income away from the ministry, the related organization must be able to conduct the business activity in its own right.

■ **Avoid excessive lobbying activities.**

Tax-exempt religious organizations are not permitted to devote a substantial part of their activities for lobbying purposes. Lobbying means carrying on propaganda or otherwise attempting to influence legislation. Lobbying is not limited to advocating the adoption or rejection of actual legislation. It also includes urging individuals to contact their legislators to propose, support, or oppose legislation. If substantial lobbying activities exist, tax-exempt status is forfeited. Lobbying activities may be found to be substantial in the 10%-20% range of total ministry activities.

Ministries *other than churches, church auxiliaries, and certain affiliated organizations* are permitted to make a special election (choice). For electing organizations, lobbying expenses will be insubstantial if they are below certain limits based on the ministry's annual budget. Lobbying expenses are limited to between 5% and 20% of an electing organization's annual budget for exempt expenses. A maximum limit on lobbying expenses of $1,500,000 applies in any event. An additional 25% of this amount is allowed for grass roots expenses, defined as trying to influence legislation by affecting public opinion. If these limits are exceeded, an electing ministry may forfeit its tax-exempt status.

■ **Avoid sending earmarked donations to noncontrolled foreign ministries.**

Contributions by individuals to any exempt religious ministry organized in the United States are normally deductible. Contributions to ministries that are not organized in the United States are not deductible. Most other countries have a similar rule, that is, donations to a U.S. ministry are not deductible in that country. Thus, contributions by a U.S. donor to a U.S. ministry that conducts operations in various other countries will be deductible. There is no limit on where a U.S. ministry may use its funds for exempt purposes. However, if the U.S. ministry separately incorporates its foreign operations to allow its foreign donors to get a deduction in their own country, it may create a problem for U.S. donors.

Suppose a U.S. ministry solicits contributions from U.S. donors earmarked for its work in another country. If these operations have been separately incorporated in that other country, a U.S. tax deduction may be unavailable. This is particularly true when the foreign ministry works cooperatively with the U.S ministry but is not controlled by it. The same result is reached when the foreign ministry controls the U.S. ministry, instead of the other way around. In these cases, the U.S. ministry must tell its donors that donations earmarked for foreign operations are not deductible. It is possible to arrange ministry relationships to avoid this problem, though. Ministries that operate through multiple entities worldwide need to be extra careful in their tax planning.

▌ Avoid any political campaign activity.

Political campaign activity, unlike lobbying activities and expenses, is not governed by the rule of insubstantiality. Thus, any amount of political campaign activity completely disqualifies a ministry from tax-exempt status. This is true no matter how insignificant or insubstantial the campaign activity is, compared to ministry activities. There are no special elections available to be made, nor any exemptions from this rule. For ministries exempt under section 501(c)(3) of the tax code, political campaign activity is absolutely prohibited.

Campaign activity includes participation or intervention in any political campaign on behalf of, or in opposition to, any candidate for public office. Although lobbying activities relate to social issues and laws, campaign activities relate to individual candidates. A candidate is any contestant for elective office at the federal, state, or local level. Participation in a campaign includes publishing or distributing statements made either by a candidate or by someone else directed at a candidate. Rating candidates to influence how people may vote also is regarded as campaign activity.

▌ Avoid distributing profits to insiders.

Another requirement of tax exemption is that no part of the net earnings of an exempt organization may benefit any private person. For this purpose, net earnings are not limited to profit realized from business activities. Net earnings also include the gross donation receipts or net assets of an exempt ministry. This rule against private inurement, like the rule against campaign activity, is an absolute prohibition. Any amount of private inurement, no matter how insubstantial, entirely disqualifies a ministry from tax-exempt status.

> **Q** The president of Christian School has a home improvement company renovate the kitchen in his home for $25,000. He claims his home is used frequently for school business purposes and that the renovation costs should be paid by Christian School. Christian School pays the bill over the objections of its treasurer. Is this an instance of prohibited private inurement?
>
> **A** Yes. The president is one of the insiders of Christian School. He has received a personal benefit from the net earnings of the school. If discovered by the IRS, this private inurement could cost Christian School its tax-exempt status.

Private inurement takes many forms, but almost always involves a ministry insider. A ministry insider is anyone having a personal interest in the activities of the ministry, such as an officer, director, trustee, elder, leader, or pastor. Private inurement results when a person who has some control over an aspect of ministry operations uses the ministry to gain a personal advantage. Forms of private inurement include unreasonably high salaries and salaries based on a percentage of donations or fees. Unsecured loans made to the relatives of ministry insiders also are a form of inurement. Other forms of private benefit include payment of all personal living expenses of ministry insiders and restricting charitable distributions to ministry members.

■ **Avoid loaning employees to nonexempt organizations.**

It is common for religious organizations to loan their employees to another organization on a temporary basis to accomplish some specific purpose. Yet, a religious organization should loan its employees on the same basis that it spends its money. The purchase of goods or services furthers a business purpose of the organization. The accomplishment of religious ministry furthers an exempt purpose of the organization. All expenses should further one of these two purposes.

Q Parachurch, Inc. is an exempt organization that operates a television ministry employing professional technicians. Parachurch, Inc. loans a sound engineer to a Christian radio ministry for a year to help get it started. The radio ministry does not pay Parachurch, Inc. for the use of its employee. Although the radio ministry is owned by Christians, it is actually organized as a profit corporation. Does the employee loan serve a valid business or exempt purpose of Parachurch, Inc.?

A No. Since the radio ministry is getting free labor, no business purpose of Parachurch, Inc. is served. Since the radio ministry is a profit enterprise, no exempt purpose of Parachurch, Inc. is served. The IRS could view the employee loan as a private benefit to the radio ministry owners and revoke the exempt status of Parachurch, Inc.

An employee loan does not serve a business purpose unless the organization is paid for the use of its employee. An employee loan serves an exempt purpose only if the receiving organization is also tax exempt. Further, the employee must be used for a purpose that is within the exempt purposes for both the loaning and the receiving organizations. If an employee loan fails to serve either an exempt purpose or business purpose of the employer, it is a diversion of assets to a nonexempt purpose. Depending on the situation, such a loan could be a form of private inurement.

12
Soliciting Funds

It was television that made religious fund-raising the big business that it is today. But few people in 1961 would have made that prediction. That's the year in which Pat Robertson launched the now influential CBN television network. It began modestly in Virginia with station WYAH as the first Christian television station.

During the next 25 years, religious television and radio broadcasters astonished observers by reporting annual revenues far above reasonable expectations. At the height of their popularity in the mid-1980s the top five religious broadcasters accounted for annual revenues of more than $500 million. Lesser known religious broadcasters accounted for additional annual revenues of $500 million. Add to these the revenues received by religious relief organizations, and the peak annual revenues from television solicitation may have exceeded $1.5 billion. Today there is evidence of a decline in donations to television ministries overall, but donor contributions to religion continue to rise each year.

Storm clouds are on the horizon, though. Religious organizations are exempt from state charitable solicitation laws, but they are not exempt from the consequences of making wrongful fund solicitations. Charitable solicitation laws require charities (but not religious organizations) to register prior to conducting fund-raising activities in the state. The principal purpose of these laws is to prohibit fund-raising activities that are fraudulent or misleading. How do these laws accomplish this purpose? They do so by requiring disclosure of information necessary for a donor to make an informed decision to give. Typically, these state laws require disclosure of:

- The purpose for raising funds

- The expected amount of donations to be received

- The expected total costs and expenses for raising funds

- The expected amount of donations to be spent or set aside for the stated purpose

- Whether professional (paid) fund raisers will be used to solicit donations.

It could be a fatal mistake to believe that exemption from state charitable solicitation laws provides an opening for carelessness or deception. If funds are solicited for one purpose but used for another, donors are deceived. Few organizations practice such deception, but even when allegations of deception are made, they are often ignored. Some organizations actually defend the practice by asserting that donors tacitly approve the use of their donations wherever needed regardless of the situation. Donors undoubtedly approve the use of their donations where needed when given in response to a general fund solicitation. But this is not the case when donations are given in response to a specific project fund solicitation. There is only one way to solicit funds with integrity and that is to tell the truth, the whole truth, and nothing but the truth.

Funds solicitation is one of the most critical factors of the integrity and accountability quotient for any religious organization. Religious organizations cannot afford even the appearance of irresponsibility in fund-raising. If a religious organization truly desires to be accountable before God and people, its fund-raising programs must embrace the highest possible ethical standards. Simply stated, this means not only that fund-raising programs must be truthful, but also that funds received will be used for the represented purposes.

Unfortunately, many donors have been burned by ethically dishonest fund-raising programs within the nonprofit sector. They're weary of being asked repeatedly to contribute large sums of money without being told what happens to it. Donors want assurances that religious and other nonprofit organizations are responsible. They want to know that a genuine opportunity for service or ministry exists. They want to know that their donations will be used wisely and for the purpose solicited. If religious organizations provide these assurances they will easily raise all of the funds they need.

Can donors realistically receive the assurances they're looking for? What must religious organizations do to provide such assurances? These questions will be answered in this chapter. First, however, we'll examine two types of funds solicitation.

Two Types of Funds Solicitation

The first type of funds solicitation is the *specific,* or *project,* funds solicitation. A project solicitation contains a representation, whether express or implied, that funds raised will be used for a specific purpose or project and no other. Some organizations solicit funds for specific projects and then use the funds for something else. It's possible that these organizations are unaware of their deception. Some may even believe that they have total discretion over the use of funds solicited for any purpose. They do not. Deceptive practices of this kind are not only unethical, but have some legal implications.

Q Evangelical Association solicits funds by direct mail for the specific purpose of building and operating a home for handicapped children. Instead, however, Evangelical Association uses the funds for general operating expenses. Has Evangelical Association deceived its donors?

A Yes. It made and broke a promise to use the money to build and operate a home for handicapped children. Evangelical Association has not solicited funds ethically or with integrity. In addition, the ministry may be legally liable for its deception, as described later.

The second type of funds solicitation is known as *general* funds solicitation, which raises money to meet operating expenses. These funds are used to pay salaries, rent, interest, utilities, maintenance and other general overhead expenses. General expenses are considered more difficult to raise than special project expenses. Some religious organizations attempt to solve the difficult problem of raising funds to cover operating expenses by seeking *ministry partners*. These donors are partners in the sense that they promise to contribute a given amount each month. In a way, a partner's monthly donation is similar to dropping money in the collection plate on Sunday morning at the neighborhood church.

It is possible for even general fund solicitations to be deceptive. Suppose an organization makes a general fund appeal for its ongoing ministry, but uses 10% of the funds raised to launch an unrelated business activity. It is true that federal tax laws permit an exempt organization to use an insubstantial amount of its revenues for unrelated activities. Assuming the unrelated activity is insubstantial in this example, the application of funds is legally proper. But is it ethical? Unrelated activities by definition serve no ministry purpose, not even a general one. If an organization intends to use any of its funds for nonministry purposes, donors have a right to know this. To fail to inform donors of this is deceptive and unethical.

Some fund-raising situations are more problematic. Supposing a specific fund appeal is made for $2,000,000 to publish a million Chinese language Bibles. The promise is made that a million Bibles will be distributed to the Chinese people. Have donors been deceived if $200,000 (ten percent) of the funds raised are used for general overhead expenses even though a million Bibles are actually distributed? Is the answer different if only 900,000 Bibles are distributed (assuming the entire $2,000,000 is raised)?

To carry the issue somewhat further, what should the religious organization do if $3,000,000 is raised but only $2,000,000 is needed? Should it refund the extra million dollars? Should it increase the number of Chinese language Bibles it will publish and distribute even if there is no demand for more than a million Bibles? Should it bank the extra money for future needs? Or should the organization allocate the additional million to overhead expenses and other current projects? If it does either of these alternatives, should it notify its donors? What is the right thing to do?

The answer depends primarily upon the promises made in the fund solicitation itself. The fund solicitation includes statements and promises made on television and radio intended to induce a donation. It includes all written and oral statements and promises designed to persuade a donor to respond to the ministry opportunity. Thus, it is important that all fund solicitations be crafted to avoid problems rather than create them.

Integrity in Funds Solicitation

First of all, having integrity in the solicitation of funds means telling the truth. Religious organizations often want to sell a project without casting any negative light on it. Some religious organizations may fear that telling the unvarnished truth about a project will discourage donations. Accordingly, they resort to personal reflections or the telling of emotional "war stories" that have little relevance to the opportunity at hand. Yet, donors are perceptive and want to know the truth about the opportunity to give. They want facts and information. Donors will contribute generously to a religious organization they believe is telling the truth. In a word, donors will contribute where there is integrity.

Some organizations are reluctant to disclose the whole truth about a project. They erroneously believe that if donors know too much they will not give. But why is this? Is it possible that too many projects are ill-prepared and lack specificity of purpose? Is it because financial record keeping is sloppy and unable to track the flow of funds? Perhaps expenses are out of control and no one is managing the project responsibly. Maybe religious organizations are unaware of recognized standards of disclosure and what the law regards as deception. If so, religious organizations who have not kept up with the public's demand for full disclosure in funds solicitation are in for a shock.

Q The board of City Church authorized a $5.0 million fund-raising program to establish an undergraduate Bible school. The board intended to use $500,000 of the funds received to purchase a residence for its Senior Pastor and an anniversary vacation trip for the pastor's family. However, it decided not to disclose these facts in any of its solicitation letters mailed to 5,000 prospective donors. Is there a problem?

A In this example the board authorized a $5.0 million fund-raising program based upon deception. The deception is serious. It is not a harmless, insignificant matter within the board's discretion. The board intended to deceive donors and in the process breached its responsibilities. The deception is found in the representation that the entire $5.0 million is needed to establish the Bible school. Further deception exists in the nondisclosure that $500,000 would be used to purchase a residence and funds would be used to send the pastor's family on a vacation.

Can fund solicitation programs be designed to be truthful and effective? Yes, according to El Ridder, President of Management Development Associates, a fund-raising and business consultant to many religious organizations. El says, "Donors must be told the truth about why their contributions are needed and how their contributions will be used. We will not be involved in any fund-raising program unless we are confident that everything stated in the fund solicitation materials is true and accurate. It pays to be truthful in every respect." What should be done to solicit funds truthfully? Here are some helpful tips:

▌**Disclose all material information.**
Do not hide anything. If funds are solicited for general operating expenses, donors are entitled to know it. Similarly, if funds are solicited for specific purposes it should be made clear how the funds will be used. Do not solicit $2,000,000 to publish and distribute a million Chinese language Bibles if only $1,800,000 is needed. On the other hand, donors will understand if they are told that $200,000 is required because an administrative charge of 10% will be assessed to meet general overhead expenses. A simple statement included in the solicitation stating that "the ministry assesses a charge of 10% against all donations to cover overhead

expenses" properly informs donors. A similar statement on the donation receipt is also helpful.

I **Verify information and facts.**

Inform donors when estimates are being made. It is not truthful to tell donors that a million people were exposed to the gospel during an evangelistic campaign if this is only an estimate. State facts and use statistical information only if verified. To merely guess, or to rely on unverified information from third parties, is deceptive. To "speak evangelistically," that is, to stretch the truth, discredits an organization. By engaging in deceptive fund solicitations an organization will soon gain a reputation among donors as being unreliable and unaccountable. Nothing should be stated in any solicitation materials unless it is accurate, put in a proper context, and truthful in all particulars. Verify facts, and avoid exaggerations and meaningless generalities. If these positive practices are followed, an organization's reputation for integrity will grow as will its donation receipts.

I **Deal with fund application contingencies.**

It is a simple matter to inform donors that extra funds raised will be used for other purposes. Yet few religious organizations do so. If $3,000,000 is likely to be raised for a specific project when only $2,000,000 is needed, a statement similar to the following may be placed on solicitation materials to make the necessary disclosure:

> Funds received in excess of $2.0 million will be applied to other ministry projects.

Donors are also entitled to know what happens if insufficient funds are received. For example, donors should be told if a minimum amount must be raised before the project will proceed. A statement similar to the following in solicitation materials will clarify the issue:

If less than $500,000 is received, the project for which these funds are solicited will not be possible and all funds will be applied to other ministry projects.

■ **Communicate with donors.**

Donors want to be informed, so communicate with them. Tell them what is happening. Some religious organizations have learned that donors will give more freely if they are told how their donations are used. Be honest and do not exaggerate results or use unverified statistics. Nothing will instill confidence in donors more readily than to receive a letter that tells it like it is without pulling any punches. If the project is a success, tell them about it in factual terms. But if the project failed, tell them that, too.

Everyone knows that not every program is successful. Some programs miss the mark because of circumstances beyond the organization's control. Others fail to reach their goals because of a lack of planning or other management failure. Some organizations simply cannot admit failures of any kind and refuse to acknowledge anything but success. The important thing is to communicate openly and honestly with donors.

■ **Don't solicit funds based on a constant crisis.**

Many of the people responding to our survey regarded solicitations by ministries that seem to be in constant financial crisis as a problem of integrity. Such fund appeals commonly imply that the ministry will fold unless people send an immediate gift, yet the same appeal is made month after month. Moishe Rosen of Jews for Jesus says,

> Any organization that makes a policy of sending out crisis appeal letters should not be supported by the Christian public. I use the word "policy," because I'm determined that before I send out a crisis appeal I will have had to put [into the ministry] all of my savings account, sell my car, and be really desperate.

Weak funds solicitation programs tend to focus upon organizational needs rather than ministry opportunity. An ineffective program tends to solicit funds by fear, guilt, or greed. Conversely, a strong funds solicitation program addresses real concerns, solves real problems, and offers real hope, renewal, and life. This is the kind of funds solicitation opportunity donors are looking for. Donors want an opportunity to be a part of a program or project that will do something important. They want to know their gifts are doing more than just keeping people employed. People don't give to keep a ministry solvent unless it is doing something to help the public. Ministry opportunity, then, should be the focus of appeals, not organizational needs.

The Problem of Wrongful Funds Solicitation

Because of our heritage of religious freedom, religious organizations are largely unregulated and free to pursue their religious purposes. Although regulatory storm clouds are forming, donations may be solicited by religious organizations free of most state and federal regulations. Religious organizations are exempt from all of the charitable solicitations laws in the thirty-seven or so states that have adopted such laws. These exemptions are based primarily on constitutional prohibitions against restricting the free exercise of religion. In this way, religious organizations avoid the disclosure and reporting requirements of state charitable solicitation laws.

Ministries, however, must not view these exemptions as a license to handle loosely the truth in funds solicitation. Nor should a religious organization think it is immune from liability for wrongful funds solicitation. The U.S. Supreme Court made it clear in the 1890 case of *Davis v. Beason,* "However free the exercise of religion may be, it must be subordinate to the criminal laws of the country . . ." And, as the recent case of *Employment Division, State of Oregon v. Smith* (1990) indicates (a case dealing with employment discrimination on religious grounds), the free exercise of religion is also becoming more subordinate to civil laws of all kinds.

Momentum is building to hold religious organizations accountable for what they say to donors to induce them to contribute. More care is now required in preparing funds solicitation materials and programs to avoid making untrue statements of material facts than in the past. The fund-raising environment is changing and the risk of liability exposure for wrongful funds solicitation is growing. For example, the terms *donor fraud* and *religious misrepresentation* are fast becoming a part of the nonprofit sector vocabulary. What is meant by these terms and how may religious organizations avoid allegations of wrongful funds solicitation? These are matters of critical importance to every religious organization.

A misrepresentation is any act by one person intended to deceive another. It includes statements known to be false when made, a promise made without any intention of performing it, and the intentional hiding of important information. A misrepresentation, whether made orally or in writing, is much more than mere puffing. It is a statement of a material fact designed to deceive another person into parting with something of value. It is the use of deception to obtain a donation, which might not otherwise be made. In a word, it is cheating.

A donor solicited by a religious organization has a right to believe what he or she is told about the fund solicitation opportunity. It is the truth that generates the response and motivates donors to give freely. But if untrue statements are made to donors or if the statements made are literally true but are used to create a false impression, the donor is deceived. The deception has come to be known as *donor fraud* or *religious misrepresentation*.

If someone solicits donations to distribute Bibles in China knowing the money will be used for something else, he or she has made a misrepresentation. Jim Bakker is alleged to have said to donors in June, 1986, "Thanks to partners like you, severely handicapped children who have been abandoned by their parents will have a new home at Heritage USA." However, there never was a home for group care of handicapped children at Heritage USA, nor was one apparently planned. Was it a misrepresentation?

Even if someone asks for contributions that "will make it possible for additional millions of people to hear the gospel message," without having any factual basis for making such a statement, that person may have made a misrepresentation. It may also be a misrepresentation if donated funds are used by an organization to pay "hush money" to cover up management improprieties. After all, such a use of funds serves no valid ministry purpose.

A misrepresentation becomes a fraud when made by one contract party to another party to the same contract. Fraudulent misrepresentations give the victim the right to sue for damages. However, courts traditionally have not viewed the act of giving to an organization as establishing a contractual relationship. Therefore, donors usually are not recognized as having the right to sue a religious organization to collect damages for fraudulent misrepresentation. This tradition may be giving way to increased donor rights, though.

For example, in the case of *In re The Bible Speaks* (1989), a donor recovered $5.5 million in donations she had made to a ministry. The church pastor is alleged to have misrepresented that the donor's gift would help free a missionary being held prisoner in Romania. In fact, the missionary had been freed several days earlier. The court ordered a return of the donation on the basis that gifts to charity can be revoked when made as a result of undue influence. The court viewed submission to a misrepresentation as showing the existence of undue influence. The case does not grant donors the right to recover donations whenever made as a result of a misrepresentation, but it surely leans in that direction.

In addition, the deceptive solicitation of charitable contributions is a criminal offense in many states. For example, the

California Penal Code punishes false representation in soliciting donations as a misdemeanor. Prohibited conduct includes making untrue statements as to the organization or purpose for which the solicitation is made. Liability is imposed when the person making the statement either knew it to be false or made it negligently without considering facts he or she should have known. Imprisonment of a religious organization's officers for criminal solicitation fraud is therefore possible.

The California Corporations Code gives a donor the right to sue a religious corporation to compel it to use funds for the purposes solicited. This right exists whenever a donation is made "based upon an affirmative representation that it would be used for a specific purpose . . . and has been used in a manner contrary to the specific purpose." Such suits also may be brought against the ministry by any member, director, or officer of the organization. Even the state attorney general may demand that the organization make restitution by redirecting other funds to the solicited purpose. Similar laws may also exist in other states.

How may religious organizations avoid allegations of donor fraud? The easy answer is to avoid making any untrue statements about material facts in fund solicitations. The following tips may guard against making such misrepresentations.

How to Avoid Misrepresentations in Fund Solicitations

☐ Avoid making any statement that is not true and accurate.

☐ Avoid voicing an opinion unless supported by known facts.

☐ Avoid making promises without any intention of performance.

☐ Avoid suppressing or concealing facts that, if known, are likely to affect a decision to give.

☐ Avoid making predictions of future events intended as representations of fact.

☐ Avoid indulging in "puff talk."

Guidelines for Planned Giving Solicitations

Religious organizations rarely compete directly with each other for funds. Yet marketplace competition exists because there are limited funds available for religious causes, and increasing numbers of religious organizations seek funds. Some nonprofit organizations, such as colleges and missions, have *planned giving* departments to raise funds through estate planning and other deferred giving techniques. These departments typically employ in-house fund raisers. Often field staff or consultants are used to visit donors in their homes. The principal target group is the wealthy donor who is capable of making a substantial donation both now and in the future through a will or trust.

Planned giving fund raisers have ethical responsibilities to donors. The following ethical guidelines will help these fund raisers avoid problems when asking donors for contributions:

☐ *Make accurate but simple presentations.* Use ordinary words when making a presentation and avoid legalese. Do not assume the donor is familiar with the vocabulary of taxes, investments, or financial planning. If the presentation includes a proposed solution to a tax or estate problem, put it in writing. It is also prudent to include a statement in bold print that tax, investment, or financial planning advice is not being given. When presenting a proposal, avoid making promises about the benefits to be received. Be sure to disclose in writing all disadvantages and contingencies about the proposal.

☐ *Avoid manipulating the donor*. As mentioned earlier, a department store heiress won her battle against The Bible Speaks to get $5.5 million in donations back because of a finding of "undue influence" by the court. She testified, "(they) worked me over and got a lot of money out of me." Fund raisers must scrupulously avoid taking any action that might be manipulative. A charity may not exercise undue influence over a donor. The best way to avoid the risk of manipulation is to deal only with competent donors. Also insist that the donor obtain independent legal or financial advice before making a decision to give.

☐ *Recognize the conflict of interest potential*. It is not possible for a fund raiser to represent the interests of a religious organization and a donor at the same time. The interests of the two parties are not identical. No matter how hard one tries, it is not possible to represent differing interests at the same time. A conflict of interest may be avoided by not preparing any of the documents the donor may use to make a gift. All documents should be prepared by the donor's own counsel after consulting with the fund raiser. A conflict of interest can cost the ministry its donation in a later legal dispute.

▲

Telling the Truth about Tax Deductibility

No discussion of integrity in funds solicitation would be complete without examining some of the tax concerns. Tax laws require integrity in the sense that the tax consequences of any gift must be accurately represented. Soliciting organizations must truthfully tell donors whether, and under what conditions, a gift may be deductible for income tax purposes. Not all gifts to nonprofit organizations are deductible. A nonprofit organization must handle the deductibility issue carefully to avoid tax trouble.

First of all, not every nonprofit organization is tax exempt. Political lobbies are not. A nonprofit organization must separately apply for tax exemption after it is formed. If exempt status is denied, the organization will still be nonprofit, but it will not be tax exempt.

Second, not all tax-exempt organizations are charities. Only donations to charities are deductible; donations to noncharities are not deductible. Religious organizations qualify as charities, assuming they are tax exempt under section 501(c)(3) of the Internal Revenue Code. Similarly, educational and charitable organizations exempt under section 501(c)(3) are also charities.

Donations to exempt organizations, such as political "action" organizations that are not charities, are not deductible. Federal tax law requires these organizations to tell donors expressly that donations are not deductible. This requirement is not met by a statement that contributions are deductible to the extent allowed by law, or a statement that donors should consult with their tax advisors concerning tax deductibility. Nor can such organizations fail to make any statement about the deductibility of donations. As a matter of integrity and legal duty, organizations must tell donors the truth.

Religious organizations should keep these standards in mind even though they do not directly apply to religious charities. For one thing, a religious organization may be affiliated with an action organization or other noncharitable exempt organization. If the religious organization solicits funds on behalf of the nonreligious organization, it may have to inform donors that such donations are not deductible. This is true even when the funds are payable to the religious ministry, if the ministry merely passes the funds through to the other organization as a conduit. A religious charity cannot make non-deductible contributions deductible just by running the funds through one of its bank accounts.

In addition, the standards for noncharities are also good standards for religious charities. Not all donations to a religious charity are tax deductible. For those donations that are not deductible, the ministry should expressly inform its donors of that fact. It is not enough to say that donations are deductible to the extent allowed by law. Nor is it enough to remain silent about the subject or to tell donors to consult with a tax advisor.

To be tax deductible, a donation must be to, or for the use of, a charity. A donation to an individual minister is not deductible, even though he or she may work exclusively for a religious charity. Organizations that have their members or missionaries raise support need to pay close attention to this requirement. Support raised for missions work must be donated to, and be under the control of, the ministry organization. Funds designated for particular members or missionaries must be treated as nonbinding preferences from a ministry viewpoint. Unless the ministry has the right to use the donation as it sees fit, as between itself and the donor, the gift will not be deductible.

Of course, the ministry may choose to honor all donor preferences, but the ministry should not obligate itself to do this as a mere conduit. Otherwise, deductibility may be lost. Therefore, the ministry should place accounting controls and other procedural safeguards on support donations. In other words, members or missionaries cannot treat ministry funds as belonging to them personally. If they do, deductibility may also be lost.

Other types of donations are not deductible because they are too intangible or of uncertain value. Generally, volunteer services donated to a ministry are not deductible. The same is true when the use of property is donated, but not the property itself, or when only partial or future property interests are donated. Deductions may be allowed in certain limited situations. A religious organization has a responsibility in these cases to determine the extent of deductibility and to inform the donor accurately about it.

The following is not an exhaustive examination of cases when a donation to a ministry may not be deductible, but it highlights some of the more common situations when deductibility is at issue.

The transfer must be voluntary and irrevocable

The essence of a gift is that it is made freely out of affection, admiration, charity, generosity, respect, or similar motivations. A transfer of cash or other property to a religious organization cannot be a gift if it is made under compulsion.

Q A court orders a truck driver to pay $1,000 as damages to Missions Board because he fell asleep at the wheel and drove his truck through the ministry's finely manicured lawn and flower beds. Is the payment a deductible gift?

A No. The truck driver's payment to Missions Board is not voluntary and does not qualify as a tax-deductible charitable donation.

As a general rule, whenever a donor may get his or her gift back, the transaction is not an *irrevocable* gift. Accordingly, it fails to qualify as a tax-deductible donation at the time the contribution is made.

Q A donor offers to contribute 10,000 shares of corporate stock to Christian School on December 30. The gift is subject to the condition that the donor can repurchase all the shares in January at an agreed price. If Christian School accepts this offer, is the donor entitled to a tax deduction for the value of the stock on December 30?

A No. The donor is not entitled to a tax deduction because she had no intention of making an irrevocable gift. She holds the string to the 10,000 shares and intends to pull it back in January. Christian School is better advised to avoid such transactions.

The transfer cannot be contingent on a future uncertain event

A donor must transfer his or her entire interest in money or property for the transaction to be a deductible gift. That is why a deductible gift must be irrevocable and not merely a partial interest in property. Similarly, a transfer of cash or property that is contingent on the happening of some future uncertain event is not a deductible gift.

Q A donor offers to transfer some debt-free land to Media Ministry if it can raise $5.0 million in contributions in six months. The donor even places the deed for the property in escrow with an escrow agent selected by Media Ministry. Media Ministry has never raised more than $2.0 million in any given year. Is the donor entitled to a contribution deduction?

A No. It is uncertain whether the gift will ever actually be made, even though the property deed is held by someone other than the donor. Until the contingency is met, the escrow agent has no obligation to transfer the property to Media Ministry. Thus, the donor gets no deduction until all contingencies that might reasonably prevent the transfer have been removed.

The donor must relinquish complete control over the donation

A transfer of cash or other property must also be made without any intent to retain control over it. A donor cannot have his or her gift and deduct it, too.

Q A donor has transferred the title to an automobile to Parachurch, Inc. However, the donor never relinquished control over the automobile and continues to use it as he did before transferring title to Parachurch, Inc. Does the transfer of title to the automobile qualify as a tax-deductible contribution?

A No. A mere transfer of title does not qualify as a charitable contribution when control over the property is retained by the donor. Such a gift is not made to or for the use of a charitable organization.

The donor must not expect any substantial benefit in return for the gift

If cash or other property is transferred to a religious organization in anticipation of receiving a bargained-for benefit, the transfer does not qualify as a tax-deductible gift.

Q A donor agrees to contribute $10,000 to Christian School in exchange for a mailing list of its top contributors. Does this transaction qualify as a tax-deductible contribution?

A No. The donor expects to receive a substantial benefit in return for his donation, namely, the mailing list. Instead of being a charitable gift, this transaction is more likely a sale. Not only is the donor not entitled to a deduction for his payment, but Christian School may have to regard the payment as unrelated business taxable income.

The above rule is modified slightly when a religious organization uses premiums as a donation incentive or sells items on a part-gift part-sale basis (as discussed in Chapter 10). As a reminder, a premium is deemed to be an insubstantial benefit to the donor when the guidelines (Revenue Procedure 90-12, Appendix I) are followed. When a donor receives an insubstantial premium item in return for a donation, the full amount of the donation is allowed as a charitable deduction. Accordingly, solicitation materials and donation receipts should account for premiums by including a statement to this effect:

Under Internal Revenue Service guidelines, the estimated value of the benefit received is not substantial. Therefore, the full amount of your payment is a deductible contribution.

However, when a religious organization makes items of a substantial value available on a part-gift part-sale basis, it needs to be handled differently. Let's look at an example.

As a part of a fund-raising campaign Media Ministry offers a special edition Bible to donors who contribute $100 or more. The Bible has a fair market value of $19.95, which is a substantial benefit. IRS guidelines require Media Ministry to include a statement, whether broadcast over television or radio, telephone, in person, or written on fund solicitation materials and receipts, similar to the following:

Under Internal Revenue Service guidelines, the estimated fair market value of the benefit received is $19.95. Therefore, only your payment in excess of $19.95 is a tax-deductible contribution.

ECFA Fundraising Standard #5 also requires member organizations to inform donors of any incentives having a substantial value (see Appendix E).

This whole matter of truthfulness in representing the tax deductibility of donations is one of increasing IRS attention. In 1988, the IRS launched a two-part campaign to boost the compliance level of charitable organizations with its disclosure guidelines. The first part of this Special Emphasis Program was aimed at educating organizations about disclosure requirements. Charities were informed of the IRS rules and asked to voluntarily increase compliance with them.

The second part of the program began in 1990 with increased efforts to audit charitable fund-raising programs. Penalties may be assessed against religious organizations for the failure to file a complete or accurate information return (Form 990). Other penalties may be assessed for promoting abusive tax shelters or aiding and abetting understatements of tax liability if an organization fails to adequately inform donors of the deductibility of donations. The IRS has gotten serious about integrity in fund-raising. Obviously, religious organizations should take this matter seriously as well.

13

Fund-raising Traps
for the Unwary

FROM AN ACCOUNTABILITY PERSPECTIVE, A MINISTRY SHOULD BE A good steward of its resources. Yet, some kinds of donations have the potential of benefitting the donor more than the ministry. Similarly, other sources of revenue involve complex business regulations and potential liabilities that may be very burdensome. Rather than accepting revenues from every available source, use prudence. Some revenue sources are not acceptable. We do not mean to suggest that a ministry should always avoid each of the following revenue sources. But each does have some potential for problems that managers need to carefully check when the situation arises.

■ **Donated real estate that has not been appraised**
When accepting a donation of any real estate, there are several things to watch out for. For example, the property may not be worth as much as the donor says it is. The donor may have had trouble

selling the property. The donor may be attempting to get a tax deduction for a sales price no buyer was willing to pay. Consequently, the ministry may be as unable to sell the property as the donor was. Meanwhile, the ministry must pay for the costs of administration and upkeep on the property so long as it holds it.

One way to lessen this problem is to make sure the ministry receives a copy of a recent appraisal of the property. As it turns out, federal tax laws require a donor of any real estate valued more than $5,000 to get a written appraisal of the value of the property prepared by a qualified appraiser. Virtually all real-estate donations will need appraisals. Thus, it may be appropriate to refuse to accept real estate that lacks an appraisal. Also be wary of donations of real estate that are contingent upon the ministry bearing the expense of getting the appraisal done. This is the responsibility of the donor, not the ministry.

▌ Donated property subject to debt of the donor

A ministry should be wary of accepting any property subject to debt. Once mortgaged property is accepted, the debt on the property becomes the debt of the ministry. If the property cannot be quickly sold for more than the value of its debt, the ministry will have to make the mortgage payments. This can put a real strain on ministry cash flow. Occasionally, donors will subject the donated property to additional debt just before giving it to the ministry. This is one way the donor can use a ministry to pay off his or her personal debts. The shifting of debt may be more of a motivating factor behind a donation than the donor's generosity. Thus, it may be appropriate not to accept some proposed donations of property subject to debt.

When donated property is subject to debt, the ministry should get a full disclosure of all the relevant facts by the donor. This includes receiving copies of any paperwork about the value of the property and the debt remaining, including appraisal reports and mortgage papers. Otherwise, a ministry may wind up holding property that is subject to a debt greater than the fair market value of the property itself. Also watch for conflict-of-interest situations such as where the debt is owed to a company controlled by the donor or his relatives.

▌ Donated interests in partnerships

Legal counsel should carefully review any donated partnership interest, whether as a general partner or as a limited partner, before acceptance by a ministry. Any profits distributed by the partnership to the ministry will likely be unrelated business taxable income. Further, a partnership interest is not the same as a share of stock in a corporation. The partnership agreement commonly restricts the transfer or sale of partnership interests. Thus, a ministry may be unable to sell or otherwise transfer a partnership interest it holds.

In addition, a general partnership interest will subject the ministry to all the debts and liabilities of the business. It is truly exceptional for a general partnership interest to be in the best interests of the ministry. For either a general or limited partnership interest, the partnership agreement may require the partners to make additional capital contributions under certain circumstances. Even when the ministry avoids general partnership liability, it may still be liable for funding the partnership to keep the business going.

▌ Gift annuities and similar arrangements

A donor may wish to enter into a single transaction with a ministry that has the elements of both a charitable contribution and an investment. One example of this is the *charitable gift annuity,* which enables a donor to make a charitable contribution and receive a lifetime income in return.

Under an annuity arrangement, a donor transfers cash or property to the ministry. In exchange, the ministry agrees to pay the donor a fixed income for his or her life and, if desired, the life of the donor's spouse. The rate of income paid under an annuity is based on studies of mortality experience and a conservative estimate of the income expected to be earned on invested funds. These rates are determined from the uniform gift annuity rates recommended by the Committee on Gift Annuities, an association of over 1,100 annuity-issuing agencies. On the average, rates are calculated so as to produce a gift to the organization of about 50% of the amount originally invested in the annuity contract.

The use of gift annuities for fund-raising purposes presents two potential traps for a ministry: *regulatory problems* and *investment problems*.

In some states gift annuities issued by religious organizations are regulated by laws generally administered by the state insurance commissioner. State insurance regulations often require reserve accounts and other safeguards that can impose substantial administrative burdens on the ministry. Most religious organizations are unfamiliar with these insurance regulations.

Funds received from the donor also must be invested to meet the ministry's commitment to pay the donor a fixed income. However, many organizations are also inexperienced in making investments to get an assured fixed return.

It is possible for a ministry to avoid these administrative and investment traps, however, by means of *reinsurance*. Reinsurance means that the ministry arranges for a licensed insurance company to reinsure the annuity contracts issued to donors. When such a reinsurance agreement is properly written, the bulk of the administrative work and all fund investment decisions will be handled by the insurance company. Disclosure of the reinsurance arrangement to the donor minimizes any risk of liability for the ministry.

Q A donor, age 65, wishes to purchase a charitable gift annuity from Evangelical Association that will return $2,400 annual income plus a contribution deduction.

How much must the donor pay for the annuity, and how much of a charitable deduction will it provide?

A The cost of the annuity is determined by dividing the annual income amount desired by the expected rate of return on the investment. The rate of return depends on the donor's age, and is set by the Committee on Gift Annuities. In this case, the rate of return is 7.3%, so the annuity will cost $2400 ÷ .073 = $32,877. The charitable deduction is equal to the cost of the annuity less its current value. Current value is determined by multiplying the annual income amount by a present worth factor. The present worth factor is set by federal estate and gift tax tables, also depending on the donor's age. In this case we might use the table for a single life, unisex, 10 percent assumption, which has a present worth factor for annuities of 6.7970. Thus, the current value of the annuity is 6.7970 x $2,400 = $16,313. The charitable deduction, therefore, is $32,877 - $16,313 = $16,564, or about one-half the total investment.

▌ Multi-level marketing programs

Ministries that have sizeable business activities often encourage entrepreneurship and fund-raising creativity among their employees. It is easy for such ministries to combine these fund-raising activities with business opportunities focused on sales made at home or the office. One of the more popular of these business opportunities is the multi-level marketing program, where people become independent home distributors for the company. Revenues from a legitimate multi-level marketing company are derived from the profit on sales each distributor makes personally. Additional revenues come from royalties on sales made by distributors further down the chain.

When a ministry officially endorses a multi-level marketing program for its employees though, problems can result. First, assuming the ministry itself becomes a member of the distribution chain, all royalties received will most likely be unrelated business taxable income. Second, by its participation in and promotion of the marketing program, the ministry has essentially changed the nature of its activities. At stake is the ministry's tax-exempt status, which depends on the carrying out of exempt religious activities. If the unrelated business activities become substantial in relation to the exempt activities, a ministry can lose its exempt status.

Another concern is that some multi-level programs are illegal pyramid or *Ponzi schemes*. In a legal multi-level marketing program, a sales person recruits other sales people to sell a product or service, and those sales people may recruit still other sales people. However, none of the sales people receive payments for recruiting other sales people. And no one gets commissions except when someone makes a retail sale of the product or service. Illegal multi-level programs are similar, but people in the sales chain make most of their money on commissions for recruiting other sales people instead of making retail sales of products or services. A religious organization should carefully investigate any multi-level program soliciting its affiliation.

▌ Payments from affinity service programs

Other revenue sources have a similar potential for problems, but have a more subtle appearance. These include a wide variety of affinity service programs, such as affinity credit card programs and telephone service affinity programs. Affinity service programs ask a ministry to contact its donors about possibly using a specific company to get certain services. Typical services marketed in this way include credit cards and long-distance telephone services. The service provider agrees to donate a portion of the customer's service fees to the ministry. The ministry finds this approach appealing because it has a potentially perpetual source of funds for which it need not incur any further fund-raising expenses.

However, management should give serious consideration to several matters. First, by rebating a fixed percentage of service fees to the ministry, the service provider may be making a rental or other payment instead of a donation. In essence, the ministry has been paid to incur marketing expenses on behalf of the service provider (by locating new service customers). This payment may be unrelated business taxable income to the ministry. Second, by endorsing one service provider over all others, the ministry's reputation is now in the hands of someone else. What happens when the donor/customer becomes dissatisfied with the service provider? Will he or she become dissatisfied with the affinity ministry as a result? Think it over.

❚ **Speculative investments marketed as a donation strategy**
Some people are very creative at finding new ways to profit personally and yet appear to be helping ministries. One kind of strategy involves the creation of a limited partnership to conduct new product research and development. Limited partnership units are sold to investors who then immediately donate their investment units to a ministry. However, a ministry may be selected only if it has been approved by the partnership for participation. The ministry then issues a tax-deductible receipt to the donor/investor for the initial investment. However, such a strategy is not as good as it looks.

The end result is that all the money goes to the partnership rather than the ministry. The investor gets a tax receipt of questionable validity because donative intent is probably lacking at the point of initial investment. Furthermore, the value of the limited partnership interest at the point of receipt by the ministry is probably zero. The ministry gets nothing but a promise to receive a share of profits sometime in the future if there ever are any. However, most partnership revenues will probably be paid to employees and general partners who are family members or friends of the genius behind the strategy. Do not be fooled by such nonsense. Any participating ministry has a real liability exposure for securities fraud, tax fraud, racketeering, and mail fraud.

14
Why Should Financial Disclosures Be Made?

DONORS CONTRIBUTE TO A MINISTRY BECAUSE THEY BELIEVE IN ITS mission. That is, donors are generally aware of what the ministry is doing and saying, and approve of it. Perhaps very few donors analyze their giving habits in terms of truth. Nonetheless, people give to ministries that promote a view of truth (on matters of religion and ministry) they agree with. Donors do not normally give to ministries holding religious or social views completely opposed to their own. In a sense, donors view all religious ministries as being in the "truth business."

Even though different ministries promote different views of truth, each donor believes the ministry he or she supports is telling the truth to others. Thus, regardless of which view of truth any ministry promotes, there is a universal expectation among donors that the ministries they support are telling the truth in some area of ministry.

This inevitably leads donors to believe that each ministry they support is also telling its donors the truth about how the ministry really operates. Donors also expect to hear the truth about what kind of impact the ministry really has, and what kind of financial condition the ministry is really in. Donors do not expect any ministry they support to lie about its operations, impact, or finances, because to do so is totally inconsistent with the expectation that truth is the business of the ministry. Nor do donors expect a ministry they support to deceive people as to its financial condition, or to withhold information that may have a material impact on its need for contributions.

Like it or not, religious organizations are in the position of having their donors expect that a complete telling of the truth, or full disclosure, is to be a prominent feature of the ministry. Why then, are some ministries reluctant to disclose fully the scope of their operations and financial condition to donors? Why is it that the public dissemination of annual audited financial statements by ministries is the exception, not the rule?

Why Organizations Are Reluctant to Disclose

The reluctance of many organizations to fully disclose their financial condition may be due to two primary factors.

Fear

Some ministries appear to solicit donations on the basis of fear. In other words, a ministry may be afraid to tell donors any negative facts about its operations or programs because management fears that donors may choose not to continue their support. Negative facts about the ministry may appear in its *audited financial statements*. Audited financial statements are different from financial statements that are merely compiled or reviewed. Audited statements require independent auditors to disclose in writing any condition, operation, or document that may have a material negative impact on the financial condition of the ministry. Thus, retaining independent auditors and distributing audited financial statements by the ministry are sometimes feared by management.

However, ministries could take a cue from the business world regarding full disclosure in the solicitation of funds. Of course, there are laws against false advertising and requirements for proper product labeling (two forms of disclosure regulation). But, more germane to funds solicitation, there are *securities laws* at both the state and federal levels. Securities laws regulate the manner in which businesses raise funds by the sale of investments in the enterprise, whether of stocks, bonds, or other investment forms.

One of the primary purposes of securities laws is to require any business to make full disclosure about its legal status, its personnel and their qualifications, and its operations. Additional disclosures must be made about how much money is intended to be raised and under what conditions, how the funds will be used, risk factors associated with the investment, and the financial condition of the business. A detailed disclosure document is required to be given to any potential investor before the investment is made.

Naturally, businesses are sometimes reluctant to make this full disclosure, but it simply has become part of the cost of raising funds. In spite of the fear that people may choose not to invest in a company once they read its disclosure document, the disclosure is made anyway. Of course, not every securities offering is successful, but this has not stopped people from making new investments, and it has not stopped businesses from making full disclosure.

In the end, businesses that are afraid to make full disclosure cannot raise funds through the sale of investments. Businesses that cannot stand the scrutiny of investors or securities agencies are left out of the marketplace. This does not mean that every business that does make full disclosure will succeed, but at least it has met the minimal requirements for participating in the investment field. This is not merely a legal requirement, but is also a matter of organizational integrity.

Similarly, the time is coming when ministries will be judged on the basis of whether or not they have complied with minimal standards of integrity in regard to financial disclosure. Of course, government regulation does not now require ministries to give a disclosure document to potential donors prior to receiving their donations. Everyone hopes such government regulation will never be imposed. Yet, the obvious warning in all this is that if ministries continue to avoid making disclosure, government regulation may eventually force disclosure. Some say that government must regulate ministries if self-regulation fails. If current legal trends continue, it is unlikely that people will let even religious liberty laws stand in the way of requiring ministries to disclose fully their financial condition.

Not realizing donors have a moral right to know

A second reason ministries are reluctant to make a full disclosure about themselves is that they may not know donors have a moral right to know how their donations are being used. While ministries are under no legal requirement to disclose their finances to donors, the moral right to know still exists. In turn, ministries have an ethical duty to inform donors of their finances. Whether a ministry acknowledges and strives to fulfill this ethical duty is a matter of integrity. As for the donor, the right to know is an aspect of his or her stewardship. In other words, the donor's stewardship depends on whether he or she has been given the right information about the ministry.

Psalm 24:1 says that "The earth is the Lord's, and everything in it, the world, and all who live in it." Even though people receive the title to a specific property by God's gift, God remains the ultimate owner of everything, because he owns both the world and people. Accordingly, our relationship to property is as a steward of God. In a sense, we hold property in trust for the benefit of the Creator. Our duty to God is to care for the property God has given us.

The most important principle of stewardship is that God wants us to put all property to a proper kind of use. When we fail to do that, we violate our stewardship duty. The key to a stewardly use of property is its use in conformity with God's will. Luke 16:13 states, "No servant can serve two masters." People will either use property to serve God for his purposes, or to serve the world for its purposes.

Donor stewardship is not a question of whether too much, too little, or the wrong kind of property is being used. It is not dependent on the rate of return on investment. These matters are merely the means to an end, namely, to put property to a godly use. The choice of means is always subject to variation and, hence, is not a sure guide for responsible stewardship. Thus, stewardship in giving is not dependent on the amount of the gift or whether it is tax deductible.

The stewardship of any gift is measured by how well the donor sees to it that the gift is put to good use. Since the donor receives nothing in return for his or her gift, no direct use of the gift is made except to give it away. The usefulness of any gift is ultimately determined by the receiving ministry, so the stewardship of the donor is vicarious. Therefore, the stewardly gift is one that enables the ministry to put property to a godly use, which could not have been done otherwise. Gifts that are likely to be used for an improper purpose, or that are made without investigating their probable use when received, are not stewardly.

A wise ministry, therefore, will work to help its donors to be good stewards. Donors should be told enough information to know whether funds are being put to a godly use by the ministry. After all, the donor's stewardship is a function of this knowledge. The ministry should make an effort to communicate why it needs gifts, and what use it will make of them. To assist its donors, the ministry should demonstrate its own good stewardship. This is primarily accomplished through the disclosure of financial statements.

Standards for Financial Accountability

In recent years, a number of organizations have been formed to promote accountability and self-regulation within certain segments of the religious community. There are two primary factors that spurred the creation of these organizations. First, there is the recognition—which we discussed—that donors are entitled to know certain things about the ministries they support. Second, many have realized that if the religious community does not take significant action to regulate itself, it is extremely probable that government regulation will be imposed. Two of the more prominent of these organizations are ECFA and EFICOM, both of which are discussed in detail below.

ECFA disclosure standards
Founded in 1979, the Evangelical Council for Financial Accountability (ECFA) is comprised of over 600 religious, charitable, and educational organizations qualified for tax-exempt, nonprofit status. According to the organization's 1990 Member List, ECFA's steadfast purpose is to enunciate and maintain a code of financial accountability and reporting that is consistent with enlightened and responsible Christian faith and practice. ECFA's Standards of Responsible Stewardship is shown at Appendix F, and the ECFA Donor's Bill of Rights is reproduced in Appendix G.

A quick look at the Standards of Responsible Stewardship indicates that disclosure, external and internal, plays a prominent role in the matter of organization stewardship.

∎ External disclosure

Standard #3 requires every member organization to have audited financial statements prepared in accordance with recognized accounting principles and auditing standards each year.

Standard #5 requires each member organization to provide a copy of its current financial statements to anyone upon written request, whether a donor, a member, employee, or any other interested person. Although anyone can request a copy of the financial statement, the primary purpose for these standards is to make full disclosure to donors of the member organization. By these requirements, the ECFA standards affirm the moral right of every donor to know how the organization is using his or her donations as a way to fulfill the donor's own duty of responsible stewardship. Disclosure of the financial statements to donors is a key ingredient to the ability of donors to hold the organization accountable for the use of donor contributions.

∎ Internal disclosure

Standard #4 requires every member organization to have an independent functioning audit review committee for the purpose of reviewing the annual audit and reporting its findings to the board. This requirement ensures that the board is adequately informed about the finances of the organization. The intention behind Standard #4 is to make sure that management cannot impede this full disclosure to the board.

Upon learning of the organization's financial condition from this independent audit review committee, the board is then in a position to be able to hold management accountable for the organization's finances. Thus, full disclosure to the board is an essential ingredient of the board's ability to hold management accountable for its actions.

▌ A commitment to moral integrity

As mentioned above, there is no legal requirement that any ministry organization disclose its financial statements to the public. The ECFA standards clearly apply in the area of moral rights and obligations, not legally enforceable rights and obligations. Thus, membership in the ECFA and compliance with its standards is an indication of an organization's commitment to moral integrity, not merely complying with the minimal requirements of the law. It is this compliance with moral standards above and beyond the minimum legal requirements that is the hallmark of integrity.

To emphasize this point, the ECFA's Donor's Bill of Rights (see Appendix G) makes repeated reference to the donor's right to obtain full disclosure. Each of the first three rights refers to something the donor is entitled to know: how funds are being spent, what ministry programs are accomplishing, and the extent of compliance with applicable laws. Two other donor rights affirm the right of donors to obtain further information, either by making inquiries or by personally visiting ministry facilities. Thus, a full one-half of the donor's bill of rights is dedicated to the satisfaction of a donor's moral right to know what a ministry organization is doing with his or her contributions.

EFICOM disclosure standards

Another organization similar to ECFA is the Ethics and Financial Integrity Commission, or EFICOM. EFICOM is a commission of the National Religious Broadcasters (NRB), whose membership is limited to NRB members. EFICOM accreditation is mandatory for all members of NRB that are tax exempt under section 501(c)(3). Failure to meet the EFICOM criteria is cause for an organization to be disciplined by the NRB Board of Directors.

The EFICOM Accreditation Criteria, reproduced in Appendix H, relate to the areas of stewardship, accounting and financial reporting, fund-raising, and the supervision and commendation of member organizations. The accounting and financial reporting criteria acknowledge that member organizations are accountable to their donors. According to the criteria, organizations are accountable for the disposition of monies received as an aspect of every person's stewardship before God.

▌ **A public statement**

An annually prepared audited financial statement must be submitted to EFICOM and made available to the public by every member organization that derives annual revenues from broadcasting ministry in excess of $1,000,000. Member organizations that have broadcasting revenues from $500,000 through $1,000,000 need to prepare audited financial statements only every other year, with unaudited statements in between. Smaller member organizations need only prepare unaudited annual financial statements.

▌ **A moral duty to donors**

The moral duty owed to donors is also strongly acknowledged. Donors of member organizations are acknowledged to be among those "to whom reports are due." Upon written request, "donors must be provided copies by mail free of charge." Finally, annual reports are not limited to the disclosure of financial information, but must include "a review of the work in spiritual dimensions of the ministry for which the funds were raised."

A Common Assumption about Financial Disclosure

It should be noted that the requirements of ECFA and EFICOM are not unique to religious organizations. The Better Business Bureau requires much the same thing of its member organizations (see standards of public accountability, reproduced in Appendix C, which apply to nonreligious organizations nationwide). Each member organization is required to provide on request an annual report and a copy of its complete annual financial statements. For any organization that has total annual income in excess of $100,000, the annual financial statements must be audited. Thus, the ECFA and EFICOM standards are the rule, not the exception.

These rules are not the result of pressure brought by special interest groups or government bureaucrats hostile toward religion. Rather, they are standard rules of conduct that are commonly accepted by all kinds of organizations, whether religious or nonreligious, for profit or nonprofit, taxable or tax exempt. Viewed in this light, there is really no excuse for religious organizations not to comply voluntarily with these same standards of disclosure. Whether an organization is a member of ECFA, EFICOM, the BBB or not, there is a uniform rule of integrity for all organizations. Full financial disclosure is not a virtue for the select few, but a sign of integrity for everyone.

In effect, the ECFA, EFICOM, and BBB standards of financial disclosure recognize there are three levels of financial disclosure for every organization:

1. Management must adequately disclose financial information and other factors materially affecting the organization's financial position to its independent public accountants. (This aspect of disclosure is not stated in any of the published standards, but is assumed.)

2. After the accountants have completed their audit, their findings are to be reviewed by the independent audit committee and reported to the board.

3. After the financial statements have been completed, management is to make them available to the public.

When properly executed, this three-step procedure will assure that full disclosure has been made, enabling everyone to exercise and fulfill their duties of stewardship.

Of these three steps, the most important is the first one, namely, the initial disclosure of financial information by management to the independent accountants. Obviously, whatever is withheld from the accountants at this stage will never make it to the point of being disclosed either to the board of directors or the donating public. If management does not recognize what facts need to be brought to the auditor's attention, the whole disclosure process is tainted. The auditors cannot do their job without having all the necessary facts. Therefore, managers need to know what facts should be disclosed to the outside auditors or accountants.

What Facts Should an Organization Disclose?

One of the best ways for managers to know what facts to disclose to auditors is to understand what information needs to be reflected in the ministry's financial statements. A most useful tool in this regard is the *Accounting and Financial Reporting Guide for Christian Ministries*, published by the Evangelical Joint Accounting Committee (EJAC). EJAC was formed in cooperation with Christian Ministries Management Association, Evangelical Council for Financial Accountability, Evangelical Foreign Missions Association, and Interdenominational Foreign Missions Association of North America.

The *Reporting Guide* examines several recognized accounting and financial reporting standards for religious organizations. Subjects covered include fund accounting, asset restrictions, sources of revenue, types of expenses, investment valuation, annuities, trusts, endowments, and interrelated organizations. It helps define when information is important (or, *material*) enough to require disclosure to independent accountants. Familiarity with the kinds of things accountants are concerned about is a necessary step toward providing them with the right kind of information.

In addition, many of the facts management should disclose to the board of directors should also be disclosed to outside accounting counsel. Such items include pending or threatened litigation, the formation of related organizations, a notice of tax audit or other government agency review of the organization, and the adoption of new employee benefit plans. Management should also consider disclosing any significant change in the way revenues are derived, expenses are allocated, or operations are conducted.

Q The president of Film Enterprises sends a letter to the president of Parachurch, Inc. threatening to sue Parachurch, Inc. for a million dollars, alleging copyright infringement. Should the president of Parachurch, Inc. disclose this threatening letter to the ministry's independent auditors?

A Yes. A million-dollar suit is a material matter that could adversely affect the financial condition of Parachurch, Inc. It must be disclosed to the ministry's independent auditors as threatened litigation. This is true even though Film Enterprises may never actually bring a lawsuit, and Parachurch, Inc. may win the case if suit is brought.

When in doubt whether to disclose certain information, management should discuss the matter with legal counsel. Legal counsel should be asked for an opinion as to whether anything must be disclosed to the independent auditors. When the organization makes a change in financial policy having an unknown impact on the ministry, management has a duty to find out if the information is material for financial reporting purposes.

It may also be wise for management to meet with the auditors and discuss matters in general terms. Sit down with the accountants and ask them to describe the circumstances when an item might be material. If management is still unsure whether an item requires disclosure, it may be best to disclose it and let the accountants decide whether the item is material. Only in this way will the accountants or auditors be able to account fairly for all the relevant facts affecting the organization.

Full Disclosure Promotes Donor Trust

Many religious leaders acknowledge that God speaks to ministries through their donors. The willingness of donors to fund particular programs or ministries can be an indication that God desires a specific work to be carried out. This does not mean that everything the public is willing to fund is therefore an indication of God's approval. Rather, it is to say that God will provide adequate resources to fund whatever program he wants carried out. Thus, donation receipts can be referred to as a form of God's provision. Organizations that adopt this philosophy are often referred to as "faith supported."

The flip side of this philosophy is that declining donations may indicate that certain programs or ministries are not meeting a real need of the public. This is to be expected when individual donors exercise their stewardship before God. When donors receive disclosure information from various ministries, they make giving decisions based upon what they have learned. Thus, donors direct their contributions to those ministries and programs that they believe to be the most important. Other programs and ministries may suffer a decline in contributions as a result.

Few organizations seem willing to accept a decline in donations as coming from the Lord, however. Management normally assumes the ministry work must continue, so another cause for the decline must be found (such as prior negative public disclosures). Thus, some managers may be tempted to withhold information from their board, their accountants, and ministry donors to prevent further negative public disclosures. However, this kind of quick-fix solution to declining revenues hurts any organization in the long term.

Public disclosures of financial dealings that may be perceived as negative by an organization help keep its management accountable. If managers know their actions will be made public, they are more likely to act with propriety. When management's misdeeds have been made known, it is easier to hold individuals accountable for their actions. The proper way for a ministry to respond to negative disclosures is to clean up the problem, not to cover it up. Any ministry that is truly accountable will not fear making proper disclosures. As Jesus said, "there is nothing concealed that will not be disclosed, or hidden that will not be made known"(Luke 12:2). Cover-ups never succeed for long.

The ability of donors to make stewardly decisions depends on management disclosures. Consequently, the reliability of contribution receipts as a measure of God's direction is skewed if donors are not adequately informed. After all, God rewards those who are faithful. "Whoever can be trusted with very little can also be trusted with much"(Luke 16:10). Faithfulness is also a principle that applies to ministry management. Management that is honest, open, proper, and accountable before people will be rewarded by God. On the other hand, if a ministry does not tell its donors the not-so-good news concerning any of its projects, then it probably has not admitted the not-so-good news before God either.

"God cannot be mocked. A man reaps what he sows." (Galatians 6:7). If management sows integrity and full disclosure, it will enhance donor trust in the organization. Donor trust and confidence, in turn, will lead to increased donations. However, if a ministry sows fear of disclosure, cover-ups, and deception, it will reap donor mistrust and a decline in support. A ministry has everything to gain by making a full disclosure of its activities and little to lose. The standard is the same both in the eyes of God and in the eyes of donors. In short, the reason financial disclosures should be made is this: there is no other way to follow the example of Paul. "For we are taking pains to do what is right, not only in the eyes of the Lord but also in the eyes of men"(2 Corinthians 8:21).

15
How to Deal with Conflicts of Interest

A *CONFLICT OF INTEREST* OCCURS WHEN A PERSON HAS A DUTY TO promote one interest but chooses to promote a competing interest instead. In the present context, a conflict of interest exists whenever a ministry insider chooses to promote an interest in competition with the ministry. In essence, a conflict of interest is a breach of the insider's duty to act in the best interests of the ministry. Most conflicts arise when the insider stands to profit personally by promoting the competing interest. However, a conflict can also exist when the interests of friends, relatives, or business associates are promoted.

Conflicts of interest are especially harmful when undisclosed. By not disclosing competing interests a person acting in a representative capacity is cheating. The problem with an undisclosed conflict of interest is that two parties to a transaction may both believe their interests are being promoted, when at least one of them is wrong. This is a matter of current concern in business organizations, many of which have adopted conflict-of-interest policies. It should also be of concern to religious organizations because they are not immune to conflict-of-interest situations.

In fact, religious organizations have a unique vulnerability to conflict-of-interest situations. This is due in part to the use of volunteers seeking to help the ministry in its business transactions. The motives of many volunteers are above reproach, yet some volunteers offer their services with hidden profit motives. Conflict-of-interest situations abound, involving vendors, employees, and fund raisers. This chapter seeks to raise an awareness of several conflicts of interest commonly faced by religious organizations. Many conflicts of interest can be avoided if the ministry adopts policies designed to prevent conflicts.

Two Keys to Discharging Conflicts of Interest

Some conflicts cannot be prevented, but they may still be discharged if handled properly. There are two keys to discharging conflicts of interest.

- *Conflicts of interest must be disclosed to the ministry.* Disclosure should be made as soon as any conflict is discovered.

- *After disclosure is made, the insider with a conflicting interest must not participate in judging the merits of that interest.* This usually means he or she must abstain from voting and refrain from otherwise promoting the outside interest.

When these two things are done, the conflict of interest has been discharged. Whatever action other people may take with respect to the interest in competition with the ministry, the insider who has discharged a conflict will not be personally liable for such action.

Potential Conflicts of Interest

Following are six potential conflicts of interest. Let's examine how an organization can deal with them.

▌When insiders have an interest in a vendor to the ministry

Q An elder of City Church owns a janitorial services company. When City Church solicits bids for janitorial services from the community, the elder's firm submits a bid. When the matter comes before the City Church board, the elder advocates for his firm although it had not submitted the lowest bid. Nor does the elder disclose his ownership of the company. Does the elder have a conflict of interest?

A Yes. The elder's first interest is to promote the interests of City Church by obtaining the best possible janitorial services at the lowest possible price. This is his first interest because as an elder of City Church he must act in the best interests of City Church and not his own interests. To promote the profit interest of the elder's company is contrary to the interests of City Church.

An insider's personal interests are subservient to his or her duties as a ministry insider when acting on behalf of the organization. In the above example, the elder promoted his personal interests above the interests of City Church. By failing to disclose his personal business interests he failed in his duty as an elder and gained an undisclosed profit. The impact to City Church is that it may have paid more than it should have paid for janitorial services. Except for the elder's promotion of his own company, this might not have happened.

Of course, the elder has a right to protect his own interests and gain a profit in his business when he is acting in that capacity. No one expects a business to operate without trying to gain a profit. Still, an insider has the duty to lay personal interests aside when acting as an insider. The time for acting in the interests of the company is when the bid is being prepared for submission. After submitting the bid, however, the insider sits on the other side of the bargaining table and must see things from that perspective.

To act in City Church's best interests means that the elder must objectively examine the qualifications of all janitorial service firms that submit bids, including his own. He must review the pricing structure, references, and reputation of each firm. His responsibility as a director is to select the best possible janitorial service firm at the best possible price. The problem, of course, is that the elder cannot objectively examine his own company. He is biased in favor of his own firm and cannot possibly examine the bidders on an objective basis.

The elder could refuse to let his company submit a bid to service City Church and prevent a conflict from ever arising. However, this is not always possible. The elder may be only a minor partner in a large enterprise controlled by other people. Thus, the firm in which he has an interest may choose to submit a bid anyway. What can the elder do to discharge the conflict in this case? Must he resign as an elder?

Q Suppose an elder of City Church owns an interest in a janitorial company that bids for a contract with City Church. However, the elder discloses his ownership interest in the company to the church board. The elder refrains from asking the board to select his company and abstains from voting on the selection of a firm. Nevertheless, the board selects the elder's company as the new vendor of janitorial services to City Church. Is there a conflict-of-interest problem?

A No. The elder made a full disclosure of his ownership of the vendor and then abstained from engaging in board discussions and voting. Thus, the elder has fulfilled his duties to City Church and discharged his potential conflict of interest. The fact that he may profit from the contract is not important, because the contract was approved by other people with full knowledge of the situation.

Yet, one may well ask whether an organization ever acts responsibly by entering into a business transaction with one of its insiders. This is a difficult question to answer. The conflict of interest that exists at the beginning of any business relationship with an insider is certain and discoverable. Although precautions can be taken to prevent the conflict, every business relationship has the *potential* to go sour, no matter how well it begins. So, there is an indefinite risk that a conflict of interest will arise later, which may prove to be very uncomfortable for everyone involved.

A prudent organization foresees the possibility of a conflict and takes steps to avoid it. Thus, an organization would do well to avoid business dealings with insiders, no matter how favorable the price may be. The fact that every person approves of a relationship at its inception does not mean he or she will feel good about it when a dispute arises. While there are exceptions, business transactions work best when the parties maintain objectivity and independence in their relationship.

This is not to suggest that business transactions should be adversarial. Rather, they should be bargained-for transactions in which each party bargains for its best interests. When the bargaining is completed, the agreement should be placed in writing to avoid later misunderstandings. Each party must be free to pursue its best interests not adversarially, but objectively. Disputes occur in spite of good intentions. It is better for all concerned when people can approach a dispute without having to worry about losing a friend in the process.

---------------------------▼---------------------------

☐ Ministry insiders may prevent conflicts of interest by refusing to enter into self-dealing relationships with the ministry as a vendor. Ministry insiders may discharge conflicts of interest by disclosing such interests and abstaining from promoting or approving any self-dealing relationship.

---------------------------▲---------------------------

▌ When ministry employees are loaned to other organizations

Q Media Ministry hired a movie production company to produce a film of the life of the apostle Paul. One of Media Ministry's employees, experienced in movie production, was selected to give direction to the project. The ministry loaned this employee to the production company for two years to make creative contributions to the film. During that time, the employee was on the payroll of both Media Ministry and the production company. After completing the film a dispute arose between Media Ministry and the production company when both claimed copyright ownership of the film. The production agreement between the parties does not address either the ownership of the film or the employment status of the loaned employee. What is the conflict-of-interest problem?

A The loaned employee has a conflict of interest because he serves two competing employers. By accepting compensation from an employer, an employee accepts the duty to act in the best interests of that employer within

> the scope of employment. Here, the services rendered
> in connection with production of the film were within the
> scope of two employments at the same time. The loaned
> employee is a material witness as to creative input for
> the film and its ownership. Yet, for whom will he testify?

There is no shortage of problems when a religious organization loans employees to another organization. If the other organization is a profit business enterprise, the employee's salary becomes an unrelated business expense. Even when an employee is loaned to another religious organization, there are problems. Who will be responsible if the employee becomes injured while on the job? Which organization will pay the cost of health and liability insurance covering the employee? What if the receiving organization asks the employee to do something that violates the personnel policies or religious beliefs of the loaning organization?

A loaned employee always has a conflict-of-interest potential, as well. Typically, a loaned employee is compensated by the loaning organization, but works under the direction and control of the other organization. Obviously, a ministry would not pay one of its employees to work for someone else unless it served some ministry purpose. Yet, what benefit does an organization derive from loaning an employee—good will, publicity, or a sense of charity? Even if a ministry reaps all of these intangible benefits, it does not help the loaned employee. The loaned employee is stuck with the very real problem of trying to please two employers at the same time.

According to Jesus, no one can serve two competing masters. In a sense, every loaned employee serves two masters. The loaning employer expects to hold the employee accountable by its payment of wages. The other employer expects to hold the same employee accountable through its direction and control. The employee must please both employers with the same job performance. Thus, the employee's loyalties are divided, regardless of whether the employers have a dispute or are in competition. When a dispute happens, the employee is caught in the middle. To whom does he owe his primary allegiance? In the end, a court may have to sort it out.

☐ The lending of employees to other organizations should be avoided. If done, however, a clearly drafted contract defining wages, responsibilities, indemnification, and conditions of employment is required.

▌ When ministry fund raisers give financial advice to donors

Q A development officer of Missions Board has just made a presentation to a donor. The presentation included discussion of the financial, tax, and legal aspects of charitable gifts. The donor is 85 years old and lives alone in a nearby apartment. She has a modest estate of $150,000 and lives on social security and the interest earned from investments. The donor is so taken with the officer's presentation that she offers to make a cash gift of $100,000 to Missions Board's new building program. Should the development officer be concerned about a possible conflict of interest before accepting the gift?

A Yes. A fund raiser's first priority is to promote the best interests of Missions Board. However, by advising a donor about the financial, tax, and legal aspects of charitable gifts, he has created the appearance of acting in the best interests of the donor. In essence, Missions Board has advised the donor to take action resulting in a profit to the ministry, which is dealing from both sides of the table.

This sensitive issue (mentioned in Chapter 12 in one of the ethical guidelines for planned giving fund raisers) is emerging in importance in fund-raising. Fund raisers must recognize that they represent only the ministry that hired them. They are not in a position to give advice to donors, especially when the donor lacks any independent advice. There is a big difference between asking for a gift and recommending that it is in the best interests of a donor to make a gift. One is permissible; the other is not.

Ministries should only discuss the financial, tax, and legal aspects of giving with a donor when the donor has independent financial, tax, or legal counsel present. A ministry agent or employee may examine the issues with a donor and ask for a donation, but all advice to the donor should come from independent counsel. Neither should a ministry provide blank will and trust forms while soliciting gifts, except to a professional advisor of the donor. Above all, a ministry must not prepare for a donor any financial or estate planning documents that are ready to sign. Otherwise, the ministry is acting in the capacity of a professional advisor to the donor, when it clearly cannot.

A ministry must make sure that donors who plan to make sizeable gifts in response to a personal solicitation are acting with the advice of independent counsel. Otherwise, the donor may be able to rescind the gift. Or, the donor may hold the ministry accountable under a theory of professional malpractice. Thus, ministries with planned giving programs always should keep the following factors in mind:

- Some donors require all of their present income-producing assets to meet on-going living expenses.

- Some donors make donations beyond their means because of perceived friendship, promised religious benefits, or peer pressure.

- Some donors are incapable of handling large sums of money, especially if recently acquired, and their judgment as to their present and future financial requirements is faulty.

- Some donors have failed to consider the financial needs of dependents and other family members.

- Some donors may intend to exert control over the ministry after making a substantial gift.

☐ Fund raisers who make in-home solicitations must be careful to avoid accepting large gifts without making a diligent inquiry into some or all of the areas mentioned above. Fund raisers should also advise donors that they should consult their financial, tax, or legal advisors before making a substantial donation.

▌ When an attorney represents two clients with conflicting interests

Q Assume Evangelical Association wants to buy a piece of property for its new facilities. The property owner suggests that both parties use the services of the owner's attorney to expedite the preparation of the sales documents. Evangelical Association consents to this arrangement in an effort to save attorney fees. Does the attorney have a conflict of interest?

A Yes. However, it is possible for the attorney to discharge the conflict by complying with recognized standards of professional conduct.

A typical conflict-of-interest rule affecting attorneys is found in the Model Rules of Professional Conduct. These rules have been adopted by the American Bar Association Commission on Evaluation of Professional Standards. Rule 1.7 of the Model Rules provides as follows:

(a) A lawyer shall not represent a client if the representation of that client will be directly adverse to another client, unless: (1) the lawyer reasonably believes the representation will not adversely affect the relationship with the other client; and (2) each client consents after consultation.

(b)...When representation of multiple clients in a single matter is undertaken, the consultation shall include explanation of the implications of the common representation and the advantages and risks involved.

The Model Rules follow the pattern for discharging conflicts of interest discussed earlier. Rule 1.7 recognizes the presumption that an attorney should normally decline to represent any client if it would be "directly adverse to another client." However, this presumption can be rebutted where the attorney fully discloses to both clients the nature of the dual representation, as well as the advantages and risks involved. Yet, this is only to be done where the risk of actual conflict is minimal. Official comments to Rule 1.7 make it clear that where the interests of two clients are in actual (not merely potential) conflict, the attorney must decline dual representation.

Whether Evangelical Association has exercised good business judgment is quite a different question. In this case, the ministry is ignoring a couple of practical concerns. First, two clients normally agree to common representation only when they have a pre-existing relationship, usually as friends. Rather than getting separate counsel (which minimizes friendliness), they may wish to share common counsel to maximize friendliness. However, unless the property owner is a good friend of the ministry, this reason for seeking common counsel does not apply.

Second, every professional feels a greater sense of loyalty and duty to the client who pays for his or her services than the client who gets a free ride. There is little or no incentive to spend time or money to better represent a nonpaying client. No one gets high-quality professional advice for nothing. If a transaction is important enough to warrant using an attorney, a ministry should be willing to pay for independent advice. Only then will the attorney have an incentive to do his or her best on behalf of the ministry.

▼

☐ Religious organizations should retain independent legal counsel to represent ministry interests and to negotiate and prepare important agreements.

▲

▌ When ministry employees accept gifts from vendors

Q The purchasing agent for Christian School is responsible to approve all outside vendor billing statements. One such vendor has offered to send the purchasing agent and her husband on a vacation to Bermuda. Should the purchasing agent accept the vacation gift?

A No. As tempting as it is, the purchasing agent should not accept the vacation gift from the vendor. However, the purchasing agent should report the vacation offer to Christian School's management. To accept the gift compromises his or her responsibility to hold the vendor accountable for submitting proper billing statements to

Christian School. No matter how hard the purchasing agent tries to be objective in reviewing the vendor's billings, the temptation will be to keep things going smoothly so additional gifts will come in the future. Although the gift is not actually a bribe, it may have the same effect.

The principal responsibility of any purchasing agent is to protect the interests of the organization. To carry out this responsibility he or she must scrutinize the billing statements and insure that the work for which payment is made has been done satisfactorily. This responsibility has the potential of being compromised when he or she accepts a gift from a vendor. The gift should be rejected, regardless of whether it is large or small. Otherwise, the agent may concern himself or herself about the interests of the vendor. He or she cannot necessarily protect the interests of the ministry and the vendor at the same time in all situations.

☐ Religious organizations should adopt a policy prohibiting employees from accepting anything but gifts of insignificant value from vendors.

▍ When ministry insiders are also insiders for a related organization

Q Parachurch, Inc. is a religious organization having a five-person board of directors, three of whom are full-time employees of Master Ministries. The president of Parachurch, Inc. has recommended that the board adopt a new incentive compensation plan to retain qualified management personnel. Two of the directors approve the recommendation. However, all three of the directors employed by Master Ministries vote against the plan solely because it is not in line with the pay scale at Master Ministries. Do these directors have a conflict of interest?

A Yes. A director's personal interests are subservient to his or her duties as an insider of the organization he or she serves, which in this case is Parachurch, Inc. An outside director does not represent his or her employer when sitting on the board of another organization. A director's sole concern is voting in the best interests of the organization for which he or she is a director. Any other interest is a conflicting interest.

This is a common problem for ministry employees who sit on boards of captured organizations, that is, organizations launched and controlled by the ministry. Such employees often view their position with the affiliate as making sure the affiliate does what the other ministry directs. However, most organizations having an independent legal status also have the right to determine and pursue their own mission. (A limited exception exists for support organizations under section 509(a)(3) of the Internal Revenue Code.) The duty of every insider is to act in the best interests of the organization he or she serves. If a director cannot lay aside the wishes of his or her employer and act in the best interests of the affiliate, he or she should resign.

16

The Coming Regulatory Storm

THE STRUGGLE FOR RELIGIOUS FREEDOM IN AMERICA IS ONE OF THE great battles of history. Many of the early settlers in the American colonies were fleeing religious persecution and oppression on the European continent. They hoped to build a new nation where freedom prevailed, but it would not be easy. For the most part, each of the colonies established a favored church as the official religion in that area. People were free to choose which colony to settle in, but not which religions were allowed in each colony.

Thus, the struggle for religious freedom began in adversity. The colonists had left the adversity of Europe, only to find it again in America. In the early 1700s, several colonies punished heresy, blasphemy, and the failure to attend church as public crimes. Of course, the established church in each colony controlled how each of these crimes was defined. Yet, the colonists did not give up and return to where they had come from. Instead, they decided to work to achieve the goal they had envisioned. Without their perse-

verance, we would not have the legacy of religious freedom that
we enjoy today.

As we consider the coming storm of government regulation in
matters that affect religious organizations, we should keep these
colonists in mind. Like them, we will have to struggle under some
adversity, and we will need to persevere to prevail. In essential
matters, we will need to stand fast and defend our ground against
all usurpers. In nonessential areas, we may have to withdraw in
order to concentrate on the essential things. In all things, we should
remember that the battle is the Lord's.

Not All Things Are Religious

The key to winning any battle is knowing what ground to defend
to the end and what ground to give up. Some things may need to
be given up to preserve what is truly worth fighting for. For
religious organizations, what is truly essential is what is truly
religious. What is not truly religious is not truly important, and
may need to be given up. As we have seen in the preceding
chapters, religious organizations often engage in a variety of
activities that are not all religious ministry. And there are organizational aspects of any ministry that have nothing to do with religion.

Obviously, people in religious ministry need to know what
religion is and what it is not. The effectiveness of any strategy for
dealing with government depends on how well an organization
understands this distinction. Similarly, the whole approach of
public officials towards religion can be understood in terms of the
definitional issues. Nearly everyone accepts the idea that government may regulate activities that are nonreligious, but the religious
things government must not regulate. The jurisdictions of religion
and government are separate and one must not intrude upon the
other. Thus, the key issue in protecting religious freedom today is
one of definitions.

The historical definition of religion

In the late 1700s, a certain definition of religion became commonly accepted in America. One of the key statements on this matter is contained in the Declaration of Rights of the Virginia Constitution dated June 12, 1776, adopted less than a month before the Declaration of Independence. Working to establish a firm foundation for freedom, the statement takes the approach that all religious duties are free from any government interference. Section 16 of the Virginia Constitution even includes a legal definition of religion:

> That religion, or the duty which we owe to our Creator, and the manner of discharging it, can be directed only by reason and conviction, not by force or violence; and therefore all men are equally entitled to the free exercise of religion, according to the dictates of conscience; and that it is the mutual duty of all to practise Christian forbearance, love, and charity towards each other.

The Virginia Constitution affirms that the responsibility to worship God and to put faith into practice are both duties owed to God, not to government. Therefore, the freedom of worship and belief (or, faith) and freedom to select the manner and form of religious exercise (or, practice) are equally part of the guaranteed liberty of religion. Religion, then, is defined as "the duty which we owe to our Creator, and the manner of discharging it."

Yet, the Virginia Constitution did not abolish the state's official church. Wanting to see this condition remedied, Thomas Jefferson drafted a Bill for Establishing Religious Freedom in 1779. He did not base the bill on the idea that government could regulate all religions so long as it treated them equally. It was not enough that government treat all recognized churches or clergymen the same, in a neutral fashion. Rather, he adopted the view that government had no right to interfere in matters of religion at all.

Whether the tax went to an officially preferred religion, or the people could choose where they wanted the money to go in a neutral voucher-type fashion, government still could not tax people to support religious teachers. Instead, the people had "the comfortable liberty" of choosing not to support any religion. The right to recognize religious organizations belonged to the people, not to their government. The recognition of certain groups was a religious matter that government could not engage in. Thus, the criteria for defining a church was the exclusive right of the people to decide.

Instead of immediately adopting Jefferson's Bill, the Virginia legislature proposed a voucher-type neutral system of church support. Jefferson's Bill was eventually passed in 1786, but not until James Madison published his Memorial and Remonstrance Against Religious Assessments in 1785. Madison argued that the neutrality approach was not enough to satisfy Section 16 of the Virginia Constitution. He also argued that Jefferson's approach was required by what the Declaration of Independence called "the laws of nature and of nature's God."

> The Religion then of every man must be left to the conviction and conscience of every man; and it is the right of every man to exercise it as these may dictate. . . . We maintain therefore that in matters of Religion, no man's right is abridged by the institution of Civil Society, and that Religion is wholly exempt from its cognizance. . . . The Rulers who are guilty of . . . encroachment, exceed the commission from which they derive their authority, and are Tyrants.

This experience in Virginia set the context for the ratification of the First Amendment to the U.S. Constitution in 1791, which provides that "Congress shall make no law respecting an establishment of religion, nor prohibiting the free exercise thereof." As the U.S. Supreme Court has held, the First Amendment adopted the same approach to religious freedom as the Virginia Statute. The First Amendment ensures that government has no rights over religion, either to aid it, burden it, or regulate it. The First Amendment rejects the idea that government may regulate religion so long as all recognized organizations are treated equally.

There is no government interest that can overcome the mandate of the First Amendment. Consequently, Congress cannot regulate the manner in which people perform their religious duties. To do so would redefine religion as a duty owed to government in violation of the First Amendment's Establishment Clause. Similarly, Congress cannot inhibit the right of the people to choose how to discharge their religious duties. To do this would deny religious liberty in violation of the First Amendment's Free Exercise Clause.

The historical approach has been shelved

This bulwark of freedom had two major impacts on how religion was defined. First, as a matter of law, religion was defined objectively. That is, everyone could know whether something was religious or not by comparing it to an objective standard. This standard was the law of nature, partially expressed in the Bible and guaranteed by the Virginia and federal constitutions.

Second, as a practical matter, public officials usually deferred to the judgment of religious leaders in deciding whether something was religious or not. People thought it was better that government should err on the side of resolving close judgment calls in religion's favor, than to define religion too narrowly. So religion was given the task of maintaining integrity in defining what religion is. The result was a tradition that gave religious organizations great latitude in defining what was within the scope of religious ministry.

However, the situation since the Civil War has changed dramatically. With the rise of evolutionary thinking in legal circles after 1870 (as described below), objective definitions and absolute rules have largely been rejected. People in law and government began to reject the Bible and "the laws of nature and of nature's

God" as a basis for defining the roles of religion and government. At the same time, and for many of the same reasons, the nation began to see an expansion of government regulation in all areas of life. Matters that were once reserved for the private sector were now regulated at every level of government.

These changes in attitudes ushered in a whole new set of criteria for understanding the relationship between government and religion. In effect, the battle has been over changing definitions. Instead of governing on the basis of fixed standards that are objectively determined, public officials today base policy on loose sets of rules that continually change, which is evolutionary thinking. Religion is no longer viewed as something that can even be defined, except as a set of personal beliefs that are sincerely held—a purely subjective test.

In addition, we have seen government throw itself back to embracing an approach to religion based solely on neutrality. Instead of viewing religion as an area where government dares not tread, it is now seen as a field ripe for regulation, so long as all religions are treated alike. Though many public officials would deny it, the neutrality approach essentially rejects the heritage of religious freedom secured by our nation's founders, because it rejects the foundation on which that heritage rests.

The result is now a general misunderstanding of the nature of religious freedom that we have secured. Religion is now viewed as a qualified right to be balanced against governmental rights to regulate. This has muddied the waters of religious liberty considerably. After all, if government cannot even define religion, how can it tell shams from legitimate ministries? If everything that can be done by people can be characterized as religious, what distinguishes a religious business from a secular one?

The modern approach to regulating religion
All of this has public officials somewhat confused. They are faced with trying to halt certain obvious abuses such as sham churches.

In addition, some people in Congress seem bent on stripping away every favored status religious organizations now enjoy. Everyone wants to draw a line that separates legitimate religious ministry from the counterfeits, but no one seems to know where it belongs. The limits of government authority, the boundaries of private rights, and the concept of religious ministry have all been pushed into new directions.

Part of the problem is a lack of accepted objective standards or definitions to guide lawmakers. If religion is completely self-defined according to whatever a person sincerely believes, the situation is untenable. Not only is there no limit to what can be viewed as religious, but there is no way to tell genuine religion from the counterfeits. Government must operate on the basis of objective standards to be effective at all.

This is nowhere more true than in the area of tax regulation. Congress has enacted various provisions giving churches, religious orders, apostolic associations and ministers of the gospel special tax treatment, but neglected to define any of these terms. This is probably because Congress believed it would be unconstitutional to define these terms. However, the IRS was still left with the administrative responsibility to apply and interpret the terms Congress had used. Thus, as a practical matter, the IRS needed to come up with its own definitions whether or not they were constitutional.

Obviously, the IRS could not make distinctions among organizations based on religious beliefs. Thus, the IRS began a search for a more objective basis upon which to define the terms Congress used. However, it did not search along the lines our nation's founders had drawn. That is, it did not refer to the objective definition of religion accepted in the late 1700s. Instead, it came up with religiously neutral criteria for defining a church, religious order, minister of the gospel, etc.

That is why we have the (in)famous 14 administrative criteria that the IRS uses to define a church, and the 15 administrative criteria to define a religious order. Different criteria define what a related business is compared to an unrelated business, or what an exempt purpose is compared to a nonexempt purpose. Still more criteria specify how assets of an exempt organization must be disposed upon dissolution, and what forms of distribution are prohibited private inurement. The list of criteria goes on and on. What seems to have escaped the government's notice is that by defining what a church is or is not, the IRS has exercised the power of government in the domain of religion.

Religious organizations have changed, too

A lack of objective standards has been only part of the overall problem. Religious ministries have undergone some changes, too. One change is that, over time, a number of unscrupulous people have crept into the religious sector. These charlatans have used religion as a cloak to cover nonreligious activities from public scrutiny and accountability. By setting up sham churches as obvious tax avoidance schemes, they started giving religion a bad name. Some of these sham churches have really been fronts for political groups intent on changing society for the worse. They believed one way to change society was to explode the favored status of religion by populating the system with counterfeit religions and religious organizations.

Another change is this: bona fide religious ministries have expanded the scope of their activities beyond anything that earlier generations had expected. To public officials, it has seemed that any activity that was religiously motivated became another aspect of religious ministry. Sometimes, ministries have taken things too far. They have attempted to shield girdle factories and laundromats from government regulation because they were church related. Occasional financial excesses and a disregard for usual business regulations have fueled the fire of public officials who are looking for someone to burn. The fact that some of these excesses were huge, as in the last decade, has only served to convince a larger number of people that government must do something.

It used to be that government deferred to the judgment of religious organizations as to what religious ministry included. This is no longer true. Now, instead of giving deference to religion, public officials doubt anything is truly religious because the true definition of religion has been lost. More than ever, public officials want to wrench the power of definition away from the religious sector to curb what is viewed as abuse. In a certain sense, public officials believe the trust that has been given to religious organizations has been betrayed. At the very least, recent religious scandals have signaled an erosion of public respect and tolerance for religion.

Sex, money, and fraud scandals in ministry have shocked the public's confidence in religious leaders. They have caused many to question the motives of religious organizations and to ask whether they were accountable to anyone. In addition, many resent the increased political activism of some religious leaders, suspecting that tax-exempt donations are being used for political purposes. Some people openly question whether organized religion has a positive influence upon our society. *We* know that it does, of course, but the public consensus that once supported respect and tolerance for religion is slipping.

Many religious organizations also engage in unrelated business activities. From the viewpoint of the public, the legality of these activities is not the issue. Rather, the public simply wants to know why religious organizations want to devote their resources to activities that are at odds with their religious missions. In such an atmosphere, it is easy to see why religion and public religious expression no longer command the respect and tolerance they once enjoyed.

The Stakes Are High

The history of religious freedom in America may be compared to a pendulum. When the colonists first arrived from Europe the pendulum was swinging high to the side of religious persecution and oppression. Over the course of the next 150 years the people struggled to regain a proper sense of balance. About the time the First Amendment was adopted, the pendulum was in the middle. However, the swinging pendulum did not stop there because the momentum at that point was very great. Great deference was given to the religious sector, which kept government from regulating not only religion, but also some things arguably nonreligious. Out of respect for religion, public officials gave the benefit of the doubt to the religious sector.

Thus, the pendulum continued swinging up the other side. As the limits of religious activities expanded, some abuses became evident and government started to act. This slowed the pendulum down considerably. As the definition of religion became confused, public officials sought new definitional tests to curb abuse. When these new definitions crossed the line of true religion, the pendulum swing began to reverse. As abuses mount, the momentum shifts from deference to skepticism about religion. Perhaps public officials are only trying to swing the pendulum of religious freedom back to the middle, but will they know when to stop?

The result of this pendulum reversal is twofold. First, non-religious activities of religious organizations may be stripped of their favored status. The scope of business activities that are defined as being unrelated to any exempt purpose will likely be expanded. Eventually all business activities may be taxed. The trend is to view tax exemption as a form of government subsidy to exempt organizations. Since tax exemption is not a religious right but a government-granted privilege, the exempt status of religious ministries may be further restricted. The same can also be said about state sales tax and property tax exemption for religious organizations.

Second, there is evidence that hostility toward religion is growing in the public sector. Religious education is becoming more regulated all the time. The same is true for child day-care centers that are operated by religious organizations. As shown by the recent surge in "clergy malpractice" cases, the courts seem to be increasingly willing to hold religious counselors liable under a standard of professional malpractice. And this is only the tip of the iceberg. One need only survey a variety of news bulletins such as the *Church Law and Tax Report* to see that government intrusion in the religious arena is ever increasing.

There are new cases cropping up continually where public officials resolutely deny religious rights, even though clear legal precedent has upheld such rights. The U.S. Supreme Court has upheld the federal Equal Access Act and the ability of students to meet in schools for religious purposes. Yet many school principals and administrators routinely deny all student requests to form religious clubs. Despite long-standing court rulings, many city officials still routinely deny granting permits for religious groups to hold meetings in public parks, or refuse to rent school facilities to religious groups after school hours.

These and similar decisions are almost always defended on the ground that they are required by "the separation of church and state." However, this has become a mere euphemism for justifying hostility toward religion. The conclusion seems unavoidable: government *is* moving from a position of deference or accommodation toward religion to one of skepticism and hostility, threatening our religious liberties.

Perhaps religious organizations will recapture public favor, but they will do so only as they can demonstrate new levels of integrity and accountability. But, at present, religious organizations need to be prepared for a storm of governmental regulations.

How Should Religious Organizations Respond?

How should religious organizations respond to this increased regulation by government?

Know what religion is and is not
Religious organizations need to recognize the difference between true religious ministry and other kinds of activities. For example, ministries should know that unrelated business activities are not religious in nature. Similarly, the laws of federal tax exemption and state corporation laws are not an intrusion into the religious sphere. These restrictions merely go with the territory of being a religious organization.

An organization gains nothing by operating in ignorance or in defiance of these rules. To do so jeopardizes the organization's exempt status and its ability to carry out its religious purposes. Though existing government regulations may seem unduly restrictive, their main purpose is to confine religious organizations to the reasons for which they have exempt status.

Some religious organizations wrongly believe they are entitled to favored status as a matter of religious right. However, there is no right to tax-exempt status; it is only a government-granted privilege. There is no right to distribute earnings to individuals, nor to have business income sheltered from taxation. But there is a right to engage in religious ministry, free of government interference, and that is where religious organizations should concentrate their resources.

Vigorously defend intrusions in matters of true religion
Religious organizations must not be lax in defending their rights. The best way to handle an unwarranted government intrusion into religious matters is to confront it head-on. Often, matters can be won with a gentle reminder that government is limited in what it can regulate, but sometimes legal counsel will need to be hired to

make this approach effective. Ministries should not hesitate to secure legal counsel experienced in First Amendment issues to appear before public officials. Litigation is often unnecessary because public officials may capitulate. But they will usually capitulate only when a ministry perseveres.

Occasionally, lawsuits will need to be filed to protect religious rights. Litigation is almost always a last resort, but not one to be avoided if the only other choice is oppression. Lawsuits can be lost, of course, but it is better to contest unlawful regulation vigorously than to tolerate it passively. Religious organizations cannot afford to be intimidated by laws that unlawfully restrict an acknowledged religious freedom. Lawsuits cost a lot, but no victory is ever gained without paying a price. And oppression is never squelched unless it is directly confronted.

It may strike one as odd that people should have to fight for rights that have long been recognized as fundamental freedoms. Yet, what is the alternative? To retreat and run for cover? Fortunately, there are many cases where religious organizations have decided to challenge the constitutionality of government regulations in court, and they have won. These cases can serve as a great encouragement to other organizations. Victory never comes easy, but it is attainable.

Moderate or eliminate activities that are not religious

To some extent, religious organizations can be the masters of their own fates. People in religious ministry should realize that their actions have consequences that naturally follow the choices they make. Whether or not religious ministries will become increasingly regulated by government depends largely on the choices they make in deciding whether or not to engage in nonreligious activities.

One thing religious organizations must shun is the attitude that they are generally immune to government regulation. An attitude of religious immunity is incompatible with the desire to do what is right not only before God but also before people. An attitude of immunity says, "we are holier than thou, and need not submit to mere human laws." Such an attitude breeds mistrust and skepticism in the public. The result of public mistrust will be oppression. In contrast, the attitude to do what is right before people says, "we are fellow laborers with others, and are accountable before people." This attitude breeds public confidence, and will result in increased liberty.

Make wise choices

If religious organizations wisely choose to do the things they ought to do before people, they will remove a large part of the incentive for public officials to increase regulation.

What choices will help remove the need for government regulation? Choices such as obedience to the organization's charter and bylaws, educating ministry insiders as to their duties, and selecting directors on the basis of their qualifications and integrity.

Ministry boards also can choose to hold management accountable for its actions rather than looking the other way. They can cultivate a respect for administrative and nonministerial callings within religious organizations and take care to ensure honesty in charitable solicitation. Ministries can choose to focus on true ministry rather than business activities, and faithfully adhere to tax laws. A choice to be transparent in financial matters and to avoid conflicts of interest will enhance public trust immensely. Organizations will avoid the appearance of evil when they refrain from walking as close to the edge of illegality as they feel they can get away with.

On the other hand, there are other choices religious organizations can make that will definitely invite further regulation. These include a disregard for corporate formalities and a violation of organizational charter and bylaws. Organizations that choose to keep weak and ineffective boards of directors who capitulate to domineering leaders will invite more scrutiny. So will choices to be careless in solicitation or in expanding business activities. Other choices inviting increased regulation include failure to disclose reasonable financial information to the public, a disregard of IRS guidelines, and toleration of conflicts of interests.

Whether government regulation of religious organizations will increase or decrease will largely depend on how ministries conduct themselves. For the most part, public officials are responsive to perceived problems. They do not initiate regulation simply to be on a witch hunt. What ministries do can affect their future, because this will determine how they are perceived in the public eye.

Accountability Will Be Rewarded

In Deuteronomy 28, God tells his people that if they fully obey the commands he has given them, they will be set high above the people of the earth and many blessings will come upon them. The blessings of obedience are then described in some detail. Following this is a warning that if God's people do not obey the law, then many curses will come upon them. Again, the curses are described in some detail. However, the curses that are described outnumber the blessings by about three to one. The bottom line is that if people choose to obey the laws over them, they will be blessed, but if they disobey these laws, they will suffer for it. Either way, people will reap what they sow.

The question is, which harvest will religious organizations choose? Ministries can voluntarily choose to be accountable and live in freedom, or they can be forced to submit to accountability at the hand of an oppressive government. It is our sincere hope that ministries will choose the better path.

Appendix A

General Standards of Conduct for Directors

Revised Model Nonprofit Corporation Act

(a)   A director shall discharge his or her duties as a director, including his or her duties as a member of a committee:

    (1)   in good faith;

    (2)   with the care an ordinarily prudent person in a like position would exercise under similar circumstances; and

    (3)   in a manner the director reasonably believes to be in the best interests of the corporation.

(b)   In discharging his or her duties, a director is entitled to rely on information, opinions, reports, or statements, including financial statements and other financial data, if prepared or presented by:

    (1)   one or more officers or employees of the corporation whom the director reasonably believes to be reliable and competent in the matters presented;

    (2)   legal counsel, public accountants or other persons as to matters the director reasonably believes are within the person's professional or expert competence;

    (3)   a committee of the board of which the director is not a member, as to matters within its jurisdiction, if the director reasonably believes the committee merits confidence; or

The Revised Model Nonprofit Corporation Act was published by the Committee on Nonprofit Corporations, Section of Corporation, Banking and Business Law of the American Bar Association. Copyright © 1986, American Bar Association, 750 N. Lake Shore Drive, Chicago, Ill. 60611.

(4)   in the case of religious corporations, religious authorities and ministers, priests, rabbis or other persons whose position or duties in the religious organization the director believes justify reliance and confidence and whom the director believes to be reliable and competent in the matters presented.

(c)   A director is not acting in good faith if the director has knowledge concerning the matter in question that make reliance otherwise permitted by subsection (b) unwarranted.

(d)   A director is not liable to the corporation, any member, or any other person for any action taken or not taken as a director, if the director acted in compliance with this section.

(e)   A director shall not be deemed to be a trustee with respect to the corporation or with respect to any property held or administered by the corporation, including without limit, property that may be subject to restrictions imposed by the donor or transferor of such property.

Appendix B

General Standards of Conduct for Officers
Revised Model Nonprofit Corporation Act

(a)   An officer with discretionary authority shall discharge his or her duties under that authority;

(1)   in good faith;

(2)   with the care an ordinarily prudent person in a like position would exercise under similar circumstances; and

(3)   in a manner the officer reasonably believes to be in the best interests of the corporation and its members, if any.

The Revised Model Nonprofit Corporation Act was published by the Committee on Nonprofit Corporations, Section of Corporation, Banking and Business Law of the American Bar Association. Copyright © 1986, American Bar Association, 750 N. Lake Shore Drive, Chicago, Ill. 60611.

(b)   In discharging his or her duties an officer is entitled to rely on information, opinions, reports, or statements, including financial statements and other financial data, if prepared or presented by:

>   (1)   one or more officers or employees of the corporation who the officer reasonably believes to be reliable and competent in the matters presented;

>   (2)   legal counsel, public accountants or other persons as to matters the officer reasonably believes are within the person's professional or expert competence; or

>   (3)   in the case of religious corporations, religious authorities and ministers, priests, rabbis or other persons whose position or duties in the religious organization the officer believes justify reliance and confidence and who the officer believes to be reliable and competent in the matters presented.

(c)   An officer is not acting in good faith if the officer has knowledge concerning the matter in question that makes reliance otherwise permitted by subsection (b) unwarranted.

(d)   An officer is not liable to the corporation, any member, or other person for any action taken or not taken as an officer, if the officer acted in compliance with this section.

Appendix C

Standards for Charitable Solicitations

Council of Better Business Bureaus, Inc. (CBBB)

PUBLIC ACCOUNTABILITY

1.   Soliciting organizations shall provide on request an annual report.

The annual report, an annually-updated written account, shall present the organization's purposes; descriptions of overall programs, activities and accomplishments; eligibility to receive deductible contributions; information about the governing body and structure; and information about financial activities and financial position.

2. Soliciting organizations shall provide on request complete annual financial statements.

The financial statements shall present the overall financial activities and financial position of the organization, shall be prepared in accordance with generally accepted accounting principles and reporting practices, and shall include the auditor's or treasurer's report, notes, and any supplementary schedules. When total annual income exceeds $100,000, the financial statements shall be audited in accordance with generally accepted auditing standards.

3. Soliciting organizations' financial statements shall present adequate information to serve as a basis for informed decisions.

Information needed as a basis for informed decisions generally includes but is not limited to: a) significant categories of contributions and other income; b) expenses reported in categories corresponding to the descriptions of major programs and activities contained in the annual report, solicitations, and other informational materials; c) a detailed schedule of expenses by natural classification (e.g., salaries, employee benefits, occupancy, postage, etc.), presenting the natural expenses incurred for each major program and supporting activity; d) accurate presentation of all fund raising and administrative costs; and e) when a significant activity combines fund raising and one or more other purposes (e.g., door-to-door canvassing combining fund raising and social advocacy, or television broadcasts combining fund raising and religious ministry, or a direct mail campaign combining fund raising and public education), the financial statements shall specify the total cost of the multi-purpose activity and the basis for allocating its costs.

4. Organizations receiving a substantial portion of their income through the fund raising activities of controlled or affiliated entities shall provide on request an accounting of all income received by and fund raising costs incurred by such entities.

Such entities include committees, branches or chapters which are controlled by or affiliated with the benefiting organization, and for which a primary activity is raising funds to support the programs of the benefiting organization.

USE OF FUNDS

1. A reasonable percentage of total income from all sources shall be applied to programs and activities directly related to the purposes for which the organization exists.

2. A reasonable percentage of public contributions shall be applied to the programs and activities described in solicitations, in accordance with donor expectations.

3. Fund raising costs shall be reasonable.

4. Total fund raising and administrative costs shall be reasonable.

    Reasonable use of funds requires that a) at least 50% of total income from all sources be spent on programs and activities directly related to the organization's purposes; b) at least 50% of public contributions be spent on the programs and activities described in solicitations, in accordance with donor expectations; c) fund raising costs not exceed 35% of related contributions; and d) total fund raising and administrative costs not exceed 50% of total income.

    An organization which does not meet one or more of these percentage limitations may provide evidence to demonstrate that its use of funds is reasonable. The higher fund raising and administrative costs of a newly created organization, donor restrictions on the use of funds, exceptional bequests, a stigma associated with a cause, and environmental or political events beyond an organization's control are among the factors which may result in costs that are reasonable although they do not meet these percentage limitations.

5. Soliciting organizations shall substantiate on request their application of funds, in accordance with donor expectations, to the programs and activities described in solicitations.

6. Soliciting organizations shall establish and exercise adequate controls over disbursements.

SOLICITATIONS AND INFORMATIONAL MATERIALS

1. Solicitations and informational materials, distributed by any means, shall be accurate, truthful and not misleading, both in whole and in part.

2. Soliciting organizations shall substantiate on request that solicitations and informational materials, distributed by any means, are accurate, truthful and not misleading, in whole and in part.

3. Solicitations shall include a clear description of the programs and activities for which funds are requested.

   Solicitations which describe an issue, problem, need or event, but which do not clearly describe the programs or activities for which funds are requested will not meet this standard. Solicitations in which time or space restrictions apply shall identify a source from which written information is available.

4. Direct contact solicitations, including personal and telephone appeals, shall identify a) the solicitor and his/her relationship to the benefiting organization, b) the benefiting organization or cause and c) the programs and activities for which funds are requested.

5. Solicitations in conjunction with the sale of goods, services or admissions shall identify at the point of solicitation a) the benefiting organization, b) a source from which written information is available and c) the actual or anticipated portion of the sales or admission price to benefit the charitable organization or cause.

FUND RAISING PRACTICES

1. Soliciting organizations shall establish and exercise controls over fund raising activities conducted for their benefit by staff, volunteers, consultants, contractors, and controlled or affiliated entities, including commitment to writing of all fund raising contracts and agreements.

2. Soliciting organizations shall establish and exercise adequate controls over contributions.

3. Soliciting organizations shall honor donor requests for confidentiality and shall not publicize the identity of donors without prior written permission.

   Donor requests for confidentiality include but are not limited to requests that one's name not be used, exchanged, rented or sold.

4. Fund raising shall be conducted without excessive pressure.

Excessive pressure in fund raising includes but is not limited to solicitations in the guise of invoices; harassment; intimidation or coercion, such as threats of public disclosure or economic retaliation; failure to inform recipients of unordered items that they are under no obligation to pay for or return them; and strongly emotional appeals which distort the organization's activities or beneficiaries.

GOVERNANCE

1. **Soliciting organizations shall have an adequate governing structure.**

   Soliciting organizations shall have and operate in accordance with governing instruments (charter, articles of incorporation, bylaws, etc.) which set forth the organization's basic goals and purposes, and which define the organizational structure. The governing instruments shall define the body having final responsibility for and authority over the organization's policies and programs (including authority to amend the governing instruments), as well as any subordinate bodies to which specific responsibilities may be delegated.

   An organization's governing structure shall be inadequate if any policy-making decisions of the governing body (board) or committee of board members having interim policy-making authority (executive committee) are made by fewer than three persons.

2. **Soliciting organizations shall have an active governing body.**

   An active governing body (board) exercises responsibility in establishing policies, retaining qualified executive leadership, and overseeing that leadership.

   An active board meets formally at least three times annually, with meetings evenly spaced over the course of the year, and with a majority of the members in attendance (in person or by proxy) on average.

   Because the public reasonably expects board members to participate personally in policy decisions, the governing body is not active, and a roster of board members may be misleading, if a majority of the board members attend no formal board meetings in person over the course of a year.

   If the full board meets only once annually, there shall be at least two additional, evenly spaced meetings during the year of an executive committee of board members having interim policy-making authority, with a majority of its members present in person, on average.

3. **Soliciting organizations shall have an independent governing board.**

Organizations whose directly and/or indirectly compensated board members constitute more than one-fifth (20%) of the total voting membership of the board or of the executive committee will not meet this standard. (The ordained clergy of a publicly soliciting church, who serve as members of the church's policy-making governing body, are excepted from this 20% limitation, although they may be salaried by or receive support or sustenance from the church.)

Organizations engaged in transactions in which board members have material conflicting interests resulting from any relationship or business affiliation will not meet this standard.

Appendix D

Bylaws

Ethics and Financial Integrity Commission (EFICOM)

Requirement for Membership.

a. Members shall obtain and submit annually an audited financial statement prepared by an independent Public Accounting firm in accordance with generally accepted audited standards (GAAS) with financial statements prepared in accordance with generally accepted accounting principles (GAAP) consistently applied.

In the event a member's annual donation income from broadcasting ministry is between $500,000 and $1,000,000, and said ministry has initially submitted a full GAAP audit, the submission of an audit every second year is considered satisfactory, with an audit or a review required on the other year.

Bylaws *reprinted with permission of EFICOM, P.O. Box 17456, Washington, D.C. 20041, (703) 435-8888.*

For members whose donated income from broadcasting ministry is less than $500,000, an annual unaudited financial statement shall be considered sufficient. The Commission shall keep in strict confidence all financial and other data submitted.

Each member organization shall certify annually and in writing that:

i.   Its board meets formally at least three times annually, with meetings regularly scheduled over the course of the year, and with a majority of the members in attendance; or, if the board meets only once annually, there are at least two additional regularly scheduled meetings during the year of an executive committee of board members having interim policy-making authority, with a majority of its members present in person.

ii. No board member shall participate in compensation decisions affecting that member; and the governing body shall avoid business transactions in which board members, staff or their families have a financial interest.

iii. The names and addresses of individual board members are made available to the Commission, along with any family relationship to other board members;

iv. Solicited funds are used for the purpose stated at the time of solicitation, except that if more money is received than was the actual cost of the project, disclosure of the use of the excess shall be made to the donor; and

v.   It is in compliance with all applicable governmental regulations; or, if an organization is not in compliance, in what manner non-compliance is occurring and what steps are being taken to resolve the matter.

b. All requests for financial support shall be made in an ethical and dignified manner.

c. The Board of Directors of any member organization shall consist of at least five (5) persons.

d. A majority of the Board of Directors shall be other than those joined by a family relationship, staff or employees. In the event that an applicant's annual donation income from broadcasting ministry is less than $100,000, said ministry shall be exempt from this requirement. Applicants for accreditation who are not exempt and who qualify in all other areas shall be granted candidate status until January 1, 1990, to come into compliance with this standard.

e. The Board shall adopt the organization's annual budget, oversee the accomplishment of budget objectives, establish and review the organization's programs and policies, and determine the compensation of the organization's officers, directors and principals.

Accreditation of any NRB member who fails to meet EFICOM standards may be withdrawn following an opportunity for a fair hearing.

By way of illustration the following circumstances shall be considered reason for withdrawal of accreditation:

a. Failure to make the required annual financial submission to EFICOM;

b. Failure to make a timely submission of any additional financial or other data which may be requested by EFICOM; or

c. Failure to meet EFICOM standards of financial disclosure or application of resources for the purposes for which they were raised.

Appendix E

Standards for Fundraising

Evangelical Council for Financial Accountability (ECFA)

1. **Truthfulness in communication:** All representations of fact, description of financial condition of the organization, or narrative about events must be current, complete and accurate. References to past activities or events must be appropriately dated. There must be no material omissions or exaggerations of fact or use of misleading photographs or any other communication which would tend to create a false impression or misunderstanding.

2. **Communications and Donor Expectations:** Fundraising appeals must not create unrealistic donor expectations of what a donor's gift will actually accomplish within the limits of the organization's ministry.

3. **Communication and Donor Intent:** All statements made by the organization in its fundraising appeals about the use of the gift must be honored by the organization. The donor's intent is related to both what was communicated in the appeal and to any donor instructions accompanying the gift. The organization should be aware that communications made in fundraising appeals may create a legally binding restriction.

Standards for Fundraising *reprinted with permission of ECFA, P.O. Box 17511, Washington, D.C. 20041-0511, (703) 938-6006.*

4. **Projects Unrelated to a Ministry's Primary Purpose:** An organization raising or receiving funds for programs that are not part of its present or prospective ministry, but are proper in accordance with its exempt purpose, must either treat them as restricted funds and channel them through an organization that can carry out the donor's intent, or return the funds to the donor.

5. **Incentives and Premiums:** Fundraising appeals which, in exchange for a contribution, offer premiums or incentives (the value of which is not insubstantial, but which is significant in relation to the amount of the donation) must advise the donor, both in the solicitation and in the receipt, of the fair market value of the premium or incentive and that the value is not deductible for tax purposes.

6. **Reporting:** An organization must provide, on request, a report, including financial information, on the project for which it is soliciting gifts.

7. **Percentage Compensation for Fundraisers:** Compensation of outside fundraising consultants based directly or indirectly on a percentage of what is raised, or on any other contingency agreement, may create potential conflicts and opportunities for abuse. Full disclosure of such arrangements is required, at least annually, in the organization's audited financial statements, in which the disclosure must match income and related expenses. Compensation to the organization's own employees on a percentage basis or contingency basis is not allowed.

8. **Tax Deductible Gifts for a Named Recipient's Personal Benefit:** Tax deductible gifts may not be used to pass money or benefits to any named individual for personal use.

9. **Conflict of Interest on Royalties:** An officer, director, or other principal of the organization must not receive royalties for any product that is used for fundraising or promotional purposes by his/her own organization.

10. **Acknowledgement of Gifts in Kind:** Property or gifts in kind received by an organization should be acknowledged describing the property or gift accurately without a statement of the gift's market value. It is the responsibility of the donor to determine the fair market value of the property for tax purposes. But the organization should inform the donor of IRS reporting requirements for all gifts in excess of $5,000.

11. **Acting in the Interest of the Donor:** An organization must make every effort to avoid accepting a gift from or entering into a contract with a prospective donor which would knowingly place a hardship on the donor, or place the donor's future well-being in jeopardy.

12. **Financial Advice:** The representative of the organization, when dealing with persons regarding commitments on major estate assets, must seek to guide and advise donors so they have adequately considered the broad interests of the family and the various ministries they are currently supporting before they make a final decision. Donors should be encouraged to use the services of their attorneys, accountants, or other professional advisors.

Appendix F

Standards of Responsible Stewardship

Evangelical Council for Financial Accountability (ECFA)

Standard #1 – Every member organization shall subscribe to a written statement of faith clearly affirming its commitment to the evangelical Christian faith and shall conduct its financial operations in a manner which reflects generally accepted Christian practices.

Standard #2 – Every member organization shall be governed by a responsible board, a majority of whom shall not be employees/staff, and/or related by blood or marriage, which shall meet at least semi-annually to establish policy and review its accomplishments.

Standard #3 – Every member organization shall obtain an annual audit performed by an independent public accounting firm in accordance with generally accepted auditing standards (GAAS) with financial statements prepared in accordance with generally accepted accounting principles (GAAP).

Standard #4 – Every member organization shall have a functioning audit review committee appointed by the board, a majority of whom shall not be employees/staff, and/or related by blood or marriage, for the purpose of reviewing the annual audit and reporting its findings to the board.

Standards of Responsible Stewardship *reprinted with permission of ECFA, P.O. Box 17511, Washington, D.C. 20041-0511, (703) 938-6006.*

Standard #5 – Every member organization shall provide a copy of its current audited financial statements upon written request.

Standard #6 – Every member organization shall conduct its activities with the highest standards of financial integrity.

Standard #7 – Every member organization shall comply with each of the ECFA Standards for Fund Raising.

Appendix G

Donor's Bill of Rights

Evangelical Council for Financial Accountability (ECFA)

Make sure your charity's standards and guidelines assure you of a "bill of rights" as a donor. You have the right to:

1. Know how the funds of an organization are being spent.

2. Know what the programs you support are accomplishing.

3. Know that the organization is in compliance with federal, state, and municipal laws.

4. Restrict or designate your gifts to a particular project.

5. A response to your inquiries about finances and programs.

6. Visit offices and program sites of an organization to talk personally with the staff.

7. Not be high pressured into giving to any organization.

8. Know that the organization is well managed.

Donor's Bill of Rights *reprinted with permission of ECFA, P.O. Box 17511, Washington, D.C. 20041-0511, (703) 938-6006.*

9. Know that there is a responsible governing board and who those
    board members are.

10. Know that all appeals for funds are truthful and accurate.

Appendix H

Accreditation Criteria

Ethics and Financial Integrity Commission (EFICOM)

1. STEWARDSHIP

Principles - Christian stewardship is the practical realization that every-thing
we have is a gift from God. Stewardship expresses itself as an integral force in
Christian life by motivating us to share our goods with others. We are absolute owners
of nothing; rather, we are stewards of all we receive and we must use such resources
responsibly in our lifelong work of building up the Kingdom of God.

For men and women especially committed to building up the kingdom of
God, stewardship heightens an awareness of responsibilities in matters of
material concern no less than in spiritual endeavor.

We are particularly conscious of the sacred relationship of trust that is established when we, in God's name and for His work, ask others for financial support.
Our obligation in stewardship mandates a fitting proportion between the importance
of the work to be funded and the magnitude and cost of fund raising.

Requests for support, besides being truthful and forthright, must be made
on a theologically sound basis and should always be in good taste to strive to lift
the hearts and minds of men and women to a greater love of God and neighbor.

STEWARDSHIP CRITERIA

a. Every appeal for funds should be directed toward motivating the
believers to participate in Christian ministries as a part of their Biblical responsibilities.

Accreditation Criteria *reprinted with permission of EFICOM, P.O. Box 17456,
Washington, D.C. 20041, (703) 435-8888.*

b. The trust relationship between donor and fundraiser requires that funds collected be used for the intended purpose and not be absorbed by excessive fund-raising costs. Reasonable use of funds requires that a) fund-raising costs not exceed 35 percent of related contributions; and b) total fund-raising and administrative costs not exceed 50 percent of total income.

An organization which does not meet this limitation may provide evidence to demonstrate that its use of funds is reasonable.

The donor must be informed at the time of solicitation how the donated funds will be used and that designations, if any, stated by the donor will be observed. Donors of large estate assets should be encouraged to consult with their own attorneys, accountants or other professional advisers. Dedication on the part of the fund raisers should match the sacrifice of the donor.

c. Applicants for accreditation must specify the basis on which they claim tax exemption.

d. Soliciting organizations shall have an active governing body. An active board meets formally at least three times annually, with meetings regularly scheduled over the course of the year, and with a majority of the members in attendance. If the full board meets only once annually, there shall be at least two additional, regularly scheduled meetings during the year of an executive committee of board members having interim policy-making authority, with a majority of its members present in person. The governing body shall avoid business transactions, including royalties, in which board members, staff or their family have a financial interest.

e. Upon request, organizations shall disclose the officers and governing body members and responsibilities and location of international, national, regional and local offices and facilities, as well as the organization's relationship with any affiliated organizations.

f. All representations of fact must be current, complete and accurate. No misleading data will be allowed for any reason.

2. ACCOUNTING AND FINANCIAL REPORTING

The very nature of religious fund raising places responsible religious organizations seeking funds in special relationships of accountability: to God in whose name they serve, and to the donors who are co-laborers in a particular work or ministry. The relationship between fund raiser and donor goes far beyond the transfer of money, as giving is an expression of love for God, and man as the giver is motivated by God's Holy Spirit.

As every person is accountable to God for his or her stewardship, Christian organizations are accountable to the donor for the disposition of monies received.

FINANCIAL CRITERIA

a. Members shall obtain and submit annually an audit prepared by an independent Public Accounting firm in accordance with generally accepted auditing standards (GAAS) with financial statements prepared in accordance with generally accepted accounting principles (GAAP) consistently applied. In the event a member's annual donation income from broadcasting ministry is between $500,000 and $1,000,000 (inclusive), and said ministry has initially submitted a full GAAP audit, the submission of an audit every second year is considered satisfactory, with an audit or a review required on the other year. For members whose donated income from broadcasting ministry is less than $500,000, an annual unaudited financial statement shall be considered sufficient.

b. Annual financial reports must be prepared in scope and design to meet the particular concerns of those to whom reports are due: namely, the governing body and executive management who have the fiduciary responsibilities of the organization itself, donors to the particular organization who are interested in what was done with the funds available to the organization, and those who are beneficiaries of the funds given, including those who have established planned giving agreements with the organization.

c. Annual reports must provide both a financial summary and a review of the work and spiritual dimensions of the ministry for which the funds were raised. The financial statements as required in Financial Criteria Paragraph a, and the annual reports as required in this paragraph, shall be made available by the member to the public.

d. Upon written request, donors must be provided copies by mail free of charge. Other parties may be charged reasonable costs of reproduction and postage.

e. Donations must be receipted with promptness; reasonable requests from donors for information about designated gifts should be met.

f. Acknowledgment of gifts in kind: Property or gifts in kind must be acknowledged accurately with no statement as to the market value. Responsibility to determine the fair market value of the property for tax purposes rests with the donor.

g. In addition to the required financial statements, the members shall supply to EFICOM information setting forth the value of salaries, allowances, benefits, and the entire area of inurement on the part of each of the officers, directors and principals in the ministry.

3. FUND RAISING

Methods of fund raising shall be utilized as a technique of stewardship that can promote effectiveness and assure integrity. Fund raisers should utilize the management technique of internal controls in administrative practice. Exclusive authority over all aspects of financial matters shall not be vested in any single person. Separation of such financial functions of fund raising as collection, allocation and accounting is essential for internal control.

Adherence to legal requirements and respect for professional guidelines are fundamental to sound management of the fund-raising function. There are as many ways of fund raising as there are many and far-reaching ministries to be funded. Each fund-raising method has its own specialized purpose and technique. But responsible and effective fund-raising methodology should never disregard the voice of the Holy Spirit that must permeate an organization's total efforts. The raising of funds for gospel works is indeed a spiritual vocation and a talent working hand in hand with the direct ministry for which the funds are raised.

FUND-RAISING CRITERIA

a. Fund-raising authority and disbursement authority shall not be vested exclusively in any one individual.

b. Ethical business relationships must be maintained by organizations with suppliers of goods and services.

c. Contracts between a religious organization and commercial suppliers and consultants should insure that control over materials, designs, money and general operations remains fully in the hands of the religious organization.

d. To avoid conflict of interest and potential abuse, no inside development staff or outside fund raising consultants may be reimbursed on a basis of percentage of funds received by the religious organization.

e. Requests for funds shall not be associated with material objects which are inconsistent with the spiritual purposes of the appeal.

f. Fund-raising appeals must communicate realistic expectations to the donor of what the donor's gift will accomplish within the limits of the organization's ministry.

g. Incentives and premiums offered by a ministry must be presented in a manner that is clear and factual to avoid misleading the donor.

h. Members shall maintain records of all fund-raising appeals (including offers of incentives or premiums) for a period of one year. These records shall include complete copies of all written materials submitted to members of the public and transcripts or electronic recordings of all appeals presented to the public by means of radio, television or cable television transmissions. Upon request, these records must promptly be submitted to EFICOM for inspection and review to assure the compliance with EFICOM accreditation criteria.

4. SUPERVISION AND COMMENDATION

The intent of these criteria is to foster high standards of ethics and integrity in raising and disbursing funds for Christian ministries.

EFICOM is authorized to accept requests from member organizations to review their fund-raising appeal materials and methods, as well as their annual reports and independently audited financial reports, in order to certify that such organization does indeed fully meet the high standards of accountability set forth above by the National Religious Broadcasters. The Commission shall keep in strict confidence all financial and other data submitted.

RECOGNITION CRITERIA

a. If, after receiving a request for review and completing its own review, the Ethics and Financial Integrity Commission (EFICOM) concludes that a non-profit organization does meet the criteria of this document, National Religious Broadcasters shall present that organization with a certificate of accreditation.

b. Supervision and enforcement of these criteria will be based upon an initial audit examination plus on-site inspections conducted either on a random basis or on the basis of complaints or other information suggesting that such an inspection is warranted. Members are expected to cooperate fully with these fact-gathering efforts.

c. NRB shall publish an annual listing of all organizations which have received accreditation and shall conduct an annual review of each organization so commended. It shall not publish any list of those religious groups which have not received accreditation nor make any comment against those organizations not on the NRB commendation list.

d. EFICOM shall obtain payment for its service in accordance with the attached fee schedule, which is subject to adjustment by vote of the Executive Committee of NRB, and may retain such accounting and/or professional staff as needed to assist the full Commission in its evaluation.

e. In the event EFICOM does not find an organization's practices meeting NRB accreditation criteria, it shall first indicate to the organization what modifications in practices are needed to meet the established standards and allow that organization sufficient time (up to six months) to adjust to the NRB criteria before EFICOM formally votes on the application for accreditation. In the event the organization believes the recommended modifications are not appropriate for its ministry, such organization is entitled to a fair hearing before EFICOM votes its final approval or disapproval of the application for accreditation.

f. All decisions of EFICOM shall be by majority vote.

g. If, after an opportunity for a fair hearing, EFICOM withdraws accreditation of an existing NRB member, the matter shall promptly be referred to the NRB Board of Directors. The Board of Directors may affirm, reverse or modify the action of EFICOM and, as appropriate, take action pursuant to Article I, Section 4, of the NRB Bylaws. In addition, either the Board of Directors or the Executive Committee may waive particular EFICOM requirements for a period of one year from issuance of such a waiver if it determines such action to be necessary and in the best interests of the Association.

Appendix I

Revenue Procedure 90-12

Internal Revenue Service

26 CFR 601.105: Examination of returns and claims for refund, credit, or abatement; determination of correct tax liability.

(Also Part 1, Section 170; 1.170A-1)

1990 IRB LEXIS 76; 1990-8 I.R.B. 20; REV. PROC. 90-12

February 20, 1990

SEC. 1. PURPOSE

These guidelines are intended to provide charitable organizations with help in advising their patrons of the deductible amount of contributions under section 170 of the Code when the contributors are receiving something in return for their contributions. These guidelines will also be used by agents in determining whether charities have provided accurate information about deductibility to their contributors.

SEC. 2. BACKGROUND

.01 Recently, the Congress expressed concern that charities do not accurately inform their patrons of the extent to which contributions are deductible. In expressing its concern, the Congress stated that it "anticipates that the Internal Revenue Service will monitor the extent to which taxpayers are being furnished accurate and sufficient information by charitable organizations as to the non-deductibility of payments to such organizations where benefits or privileges are received in return, so that taxpayers can correctly compute their Federal income tax liability." H.R. Rep. No. 100-391, 100th Cong., 1st Sess. 1608 (1987).

.02 In August 1988, the Service sent Publication 1391, Deductibility of Payments Made to Charities Conducting Fund-Raising Events, to over 400,000 charities. Publication 1391 contains a message from the Commissioner of the Internal Revenue Service asking charities for help in informing contributors more accurately about the deductibility of contributions made in connection with fund-raising events and programs.

.03 Publication 1391 also contains a copy of Rev. Rul. 67-246, 1967-2 C.B. 104, which discusses the rules that apply in determining the amount of a charitable contribution under section 170 of the Code when something of value is received in return for the contribution. Rev. Rul. 67-246 also sets forth a simple procedure that charities can use to provide "accurate and sufficient" information to their contributors.

.04 Rev. Rul. 67-246 asks charities to determine the fair market value of the benefits offered for contributions in advance of a solicitation and to state in the solicitation and in tickets, receipts, or other documents issued in connection with a contribution how much is deductible under section 170 of the Code and how much is not. If charities are unable to make an exact determination of the fair market value of the benefits, Rev. Rul. 67-246 indicates that they should use a reasonable estimate of fair market value.

.05 Many charities have suggested that this determination is difficult or burdensome particularly in the case of small items or other benefits that are of token value in relation to the amount contributed. The Service has determined that a benefit may be so inconsequential or insubstantial that the full amount of a contribution is deductible under section 170 of the Code. Under the following guidelines, charities offering certain small items or other benefits of token value may treat the benefits as having insubstantial value so that they may advise contributors that contributions are fully deductible under section 170.

SEC. 3. GUIDELINES

.01 Benefits received in connection with a payment to a charity will be considered to have insubstantial fair market value for purposes of advising patrons if the requirements of paragraphs 1 and 2 are met:

1. The payment occurs in the context of a fund-raising campaign in which the charity informs patrons how much of their payment is a deductible contribution, and either

2. (a) The fair market value of all of the benefits received in connection with the payment, is not more than 2 percent of the payment, or $50, whichever is less, or (b) The payment is $25 (adjusted for inflation as described below) or more and the only benefits received in connection with the payment are token items (bookmarks, calendars, key chains, mugs, posters, tee shirts, etc.) bearing the organization's name or logo. The cost (as opposed to fair market value) of all of the benefits received by a donor must, in the aggregate, be within the limits established for "low cost articles" under section 513(h)(2) of the Code. (Generally, under section 170, the deductible amount of a contribution is determined by taking into account the fair market value, not the cost to the charity, of any benefits received in return. For administrative reasons, however, in the limited circumstances of this subparagraph, the cost to the charity may be used in determining whether the benefits are insubstantial.)

.02 For purposes of paragraph 1 of section 3.01, above, a qualifying fund-raising campaign is one designed to raise tax-deductible contributions, in which the charity determines the fair market value of the benefits offered in return for contributions (using a reasonable estimate if an exact determination is not possible), and states in its solicitations (whether written, broadcast, telephoned, or in person) — as well as in tickets, receipts, or other documents issued in connection with contributions — how much is deductible under section 170 of the Code and how much is not. If a charity is providing only insubstantial benefits in return for a payment, fund-raising materials should include a statement to the effect that: "Under Internal Revenue Service guidelines the estimated value of [the benefits received] is not substantial; therefore, the full amount of your payment is a deductible contribution."

.03 There may be situations in which it is impractical to state in every solicitation how much of a payment is deductible. For example, where a nonprofit broadcasting organization offers a number of premiums in an on-air fund-raising announcement, it may be unduly cumbersome to include information on the fair market value of each premium. If a charity believes that stating how much is deductible in every statement is impractical, it may seek a ruling from the Service concerning an alternative procedure. The Service will rule on whether the alternative procedure meets the Congressionally mandated goal of providing accurate and sufficient information to contributors. See Rev. Proc. 90-4, 1990-2 I.R.B. 15.

.04 For purposes of paragraph 2 of section 3.01, above, newsletters or program guides (other than commercial quality publications) will be treated as if they do not have a measurable fair market value or cost if their primary purpose is to inform members about the activities of an organization and if they are not available to nonmembers by paid subscription or through newsstand sales. Whether a publication is considered a commercial quality publication depends upon all of the facts and circumstances. Generally, publications that contain articles written for compensation and that accept advertising will be treated as commercial quality publications having measurable fair market value or cost. Professional journals (whether or not articles are written for compensation and advertising is accepted) will normally be treated as commercial quality publications. For purposes of subparagraph (b) of paragraph 2, the cost of a commercial quality publication includes the costs of production and distribution and must be computed without regard to income from advertising or newsstand or subscription sales.

.05 In applying paragraph 2, the total amount of a pledge payable in installments will be considered to be the amount of the payment. Also, benefits provided by charities in the form of cash or its equivalent will never be considered insubstantial.

.06 For purposes subparagraph (b) of paragraph 2, an item is a "low cost article" under section 513(h)(2) of the Code if its cost does not exceed $5, increased for years after 1987 by a cost-of-living adjustment under section 1(f)(3). The $25 payment required in subparagraph (b) of paragraph 2 must also be increased, in the same manner. For calendar year 1990, the cost of a "low cost article" under section 513(h)(2) cannot exceed $5.45. The adjusted required payment is $27.26. See Rev. Proc. 90-7, 1990-3 I.R.B. 8.

.07 For purposes of subparagraph (b) of paragraph 2, if items offered to contributors are donated to the charity or if services are donated in connection with the production of an item, the cost "to the organization" for purposes of section 513(h)(2) of the Code will be a reasonable estimate of the amount the organization would have to pay for the items or services in question.

.08 These guidelines describe a safe harbor; depending on the facts in each case, benefits received in connection with contributions may be "insubstantial" even if they do not meet these guidelines.

SEC. 4. EXAMPLES

The following examples illustrate the application of the guidelines. In each example, it is assumed that the charity is engaged in a fund-raising campaign which informs patrons how much of their payment is tax deductible as required by paragraph 1 of section 3.01:

Example 1. A zoo gives its patrons lapel pins reading "Friends of the Small City Zoo" in return for payments of $15. The fair market value of the lapel pin is $.25. Since the fair market value of the pin is less than 2 percent of the payment (and the fair market value of the pin is less than $50), the zoo may advise its patrons that the full amount of the payment is a deductible contribution.

Example 2. Assume the same facts as Example 1., except that the zoo also sends patrons a newsletter the primary purpose of which is to inform members about the activities of the zoo. The newsletter is not available to nonmembers by paid subscription or through newsstand sales. Moreover, it is not a "commercial quality publication" as described in section 3.04, above. Since the newsletter has no fair market value for purposes of paragraph 2, and since the fair market value of the pin is less than 2 percent of the payment (and less than $50), the zoo may advise its patrons that the full amount of the payment is a deductible contribution.

Example 3. For a payment of $15, a museum sends its patrons a bulletin the primary purpose of which is to inform members about coming events at the museum. The bulletin is not available to nonmembers by paid subscription or through newsstand sales. The bulletin is written by a salaried staff member at the museum, but it accepts no advertising. It is printed on magazine quality paper and it is distributed on a quarterly basis. Under the facts and circumstances, the bulletin is not a "commercial quality publication" as described in section 3.04, above. Since the bulletin has no fair market value for purposes of paragraph 2 the museum may advise its patrons that the full amount of the payment is a deductible contribution.

Example 4. In 1990, a nonprofit broadcast organization sends its patrons a listener's guide for one year in return for a contribution of $30. The cost of production and distribution of the listener's guide is $4 per year per patron and its fair market value is $6. The listener's guide is not available to nonmembers by paid subscription or through newsstand sales. It is written by a salaried staff member at the broadcast organization and it accepts advertising. The listener's guide, therefore, is a "commercial quality publication" as described in section 3.04, above. However, since the cost of the listener's guide is $4 and it is received in return for a contribution of $30, the broadcast organization may advise its patrons that the full amount of the payment is a deductible contribution.

Example 5. Assume the same facts as Example 4, except that the non-profit broadcast organization also gives its patrons a coffee mug with the organization's logo. The cost of a mug to the organization is $3. Its fair market value is $5. Since the listener's guide costs $4 and the coffee mug costs $3, their aggregate cost exceeds the 1990 limit of section 513(h)(2) of $5.45. The organization should inform its patrons that $19 of their contribution is deductible and $11 is not. The result would be the same even if these benefits were received separately in return for two separate contributions of $30 each. Under section 513(h)(2), the cost of all the low cost items received in one year is aggregated in determining whether the limit is exceeded.

SEC. 5. EFFECT ON OTHER DOCUMENTS

Rev. Rul. 67-246, 1967-2 C.B. 104 is amplified.

SEC. 6. DRAFTING INFORMATION

The principal author of this revenue procedure is David W. Jones of the Exempt Organizations Technical Division. For further information regarding this notice contact Mr. Jones on (202) 343-8900 (not a toll-free number).

Index